Detours

Detours

Travel and the
Ethics of Research
in the Global South

EDITED BY
M. Bianet Castellanos

THE UNIVERSITY OF
ARIZONA PRESS
TUCSON

The University of Arizona Press
www.uapress.arizona.edu

ISBN-13: 978-0-8165-3998-7 (paper)

Cover design by Leigh McDonald
Cover photo: *Clavadista in the sky* by Rodrigo Vázquez / rodorod.com

Publication of this book is made possible in part by a subsidy from an Imagine Fund Annual Award
provided by the University of Minnesota's Office of the Executive Vice President and Provost.

Library of Congress Cataloging-in-Publication Data are available at the Library of Congress.

Printed in the United States of America
♾ This paper meets the requirements of ANSI/NISO Z39.48-1992 (Permanence of Paper).

Contents

Acknowledgments

We have many people to thank for the making of this book. We begin by conveying our immense gratitude to the people, families, and communities who shared their lives, tribulations, and affection as we toured, traveled, and researched throughout Latin America and the Caribbean. By exposing their vulnerability, the contributors to this book remind us that the personal is always political. Thank you for sharing your intimate thoughts, fears, desires. Your astute analyses will help illuminate the political and economic shifts taking place in Latin America and the Caribbean.

The idea for this book emerged from a conversation between Bianet Castellanos and historian Andrew Grant Wood. In 2011, Drew reached out to Bianet to ask if she was interested in working on a book on tourism. Bianet was in the midst of preparing a new course, "Americans Abroad," which would provide students planning to study abroad with an overview of empire, power, and privilege. Inspired by her mentors Ruth Behar and Renato Rosaldo, Bianet sought course materials that included personal reflections on travel and research abroad. She proposed the idea of producing a book centered on reflexive essays on travel and tourism. Drew was excited by the idea because it built on the book he had coedited with Dina Berger, *Holiday in Mexico: Critical Reflections on Tourism and Tourist Encounters*. We thank Drew for believing in this project and serving as coeditor for the first draft of the manuscript. Drew was unable to see this project to its completion, but he was instrumental in shaping its content and list of contributors.

Our editor, Allyson Carter, and her staff at the University of Arizona Press have been amazing. Allyson provided unflagging support, especially when this project stalled several times. Anonymous reviewers provided thoughtful and stimulating comments. Research assistants from the University of Minnesota were indispensable aides. With great cheer, Tenzin Dhakong, Elizabeth Ener, and Isaac Lanan did the grunt work, from photocopying to library searches, that is an essential part of publishing a book. Vanessa Guzman worked diligently to format the book in time to meet our publication deadline.

Publishing this book was made possible with the support of the Imagine Faculty Fund at the University of Minnesota. Rodrigo Vásquez provided the beautiful photograph adorning the cover.

We would be remiss to not include the following personal acknowledgments.

As always, Bianet is indebted to the Maya community of "Kuchmil." For making space for a Mexican immigrant turned Chicana, she thanks Gloria Anzaldúa, Ruth Behar, and Renato Rosaldo. Conversations and collaboration with Drew Wood at the beginning of this project inspired the questions guiding the introduction. She is grateful to Lourdes Gutiérrez Nájera, David Karjanen, Jennifer Pierce, and Patricia Zavella for critically engaging her ideas for this book. Adriana Estill, Christina Ewig, Lisa Hilbink, Olga Herrera, Lourdes Gutiérrez Nájera, David Karjanen, Desirée Martín, Louis Mendoza, Rose Miron, Lorena Muñoz, Mario Obando Jr., Yolanda Padilla, Soham Patel, Jimmy Patiño, and Sasha Suarez provided critical feedback. The title for her chapter "Postcards from Cancún" was suggested by Yolanda Padilla. She thanks the staff in American studies for their graciousness in handling copying and printing requests. David, Ben, and Lucía make it all worthwhile.

Barbara Kastelein is grateful to all the members of the Acapulco Cliff Diver Association (Clavadistas Profesionales de La Quebrada), including Consuelo Balderas and Yadira Placencia. Special acknowledgments must go to veteran cliff diver Ignacio Sánchez and association spokesman Jorge Mónico Ramírez. She would also like to thank the women of the cliff diver community—especially Iris Selene Alvarez and her extended family—who made her feel welcome, despite her many blunders. Also thanks to Yves Milord of Canada for his shining example of the international sports community at its best, and his support of women divers.

Misha Klein thanks Bianet Castellanos and Drew Wood for the invitation to write this essay and for providing the opportunity to explore lessons learned from a life lived crossing borders, and Bianet in particular for fiercely insightful editing and tremendous forbearance. Many thanks are due to Mandy Minks, fellow Latin American transmigrant, for her deep reading and encouragement; to Naomi Leite for her expertise in tourism studies and timely feedback; and to Cecilia de Mello e Souza for accompanying her on this journey, from here to there and from there to here. Finally, she thanks her transnational family, and her temporary family, for being the reason for it all, and her current family—Sean O'Neill and Theo O'Neill Klein—for finally giving her solid ground.

Ellen Moodie and Leigh Binford wish to acknowledge the support of the National Science Foundation under Grant No. BCS-0962643 from the Cultural Anthropology Program, as well as a grant from the University of Illinois Research Board. They thank the members of the community of El Mozote in northern Morazán, El Salvador, who shared their stories with visitors. They are also grateful to Rafael Alarcon, and to Bianet Castellanos and Andrew Wood for the invitation to write the chapter.

Juan Antonio Flores Martos expresses his gratitude to Bianet Castellanos, Iñaki Domínguez Gregorio, and Andrew Grant Wood for translating his essay into English. He acknowledges the financial support of project I+D (HAR2011-25988) "Los pueblos indígenas y la modernidad en América Latina" (2012–14). He owes a debt of gratitude to Mexican anthropologist Teresa Valdivia Dounce for providing support and life lessons.

Fernando de Sousa Rocha would like to thank Maristela Pessoa for accompanying him in journeys around the different places (and nations) that make up Rio de Janeiro.

Detours

Introduction

M. BIANET CASTELLANOS

Over two decades ago, Edward Said warned us against "cultural imperialism" and the myriad ways that imperial legacies influence contemporary cultural and intellectual formations. "Imperialism's culture," Said (1993, xxii) astutely noted, is never "invisible" but rather constitutes a shared, common experience that leaves us with the task of "describ[ing] it as pertaining" to the colonized as well as the colonizer. Yet cultural imperialism, with its reliance on a false sense of objectivity and social typologies, continues to seep into intellectual discussions of the so-called Global South to (un)intentionally produce global spectacles. Journalist Amy Wilentz (2013) calls attention to this predicament in her interrogation of the neocolonial presence of American missions and NGOs in Haiti. Over time the convergence of imperial aspirations, goodwill missions, and media coverage has reduced Haiti and Haitians to spectacles of misery, violence, and humanity. The heavy influx of international volunteers who traveled to Haiti just after the 2010 earthquake prompted Wilentz (2013, 33) to ask, "What did we think we were doing here? . . . What would we do for Haiti, if anything, and conversely, what did Haiti do for us? What kept us here? Why did some of us come back, and back again and again? Like me."[1] By asking why she keeps coming back to Haiti, Wilentz marks her complicity in producing this global spectacle.

This book grapples with legacies of cultural imperialism through critical, personal reflections of travel and tourism by scholars and journalists. Inspired by Wilentz's query of what keeps us coming back, it examines the *politics of return*—a term I use to describe the concatenation of experiences made possible by (re)visiting a field site over extended periods of time—of scholars and journalists who have spent decades working in and writing about Latin America and the Caribbean. I begin with a note of caution: we are not concerned with telling a story of enlightenment and goodwill. Instead, we focus on the moments, slippages, and conundrums that left a deep mark on us and caused us to question our intentions and intellectual commitments. We consider how first encounters—those initial, awkward attempts to learn about a culture and a people—evolved into enduring and critical engagements. This book claims that returns are political. By returning again and again to a particular place, we became aware of the pervasive and insidious ways that empire shapes the everyday and the spectacular. The imprint of these encounters and returns has transformed us and our research, and yet these experiences and insights are often excised from our scholarly work. We reflect on these encounters and returns to illuminate the vicissitudes involved in producing "objective" research and leading study abroad programs. As we contemplate the ethics and racial politics of traveling and doing research abroad, we call attention to the power and privilege that permit us to enter people's lives, ask intimate questions, and publish these disclosures. As Pierre Bourdieu and colleagues (1999, 1) advise, "making *private* worlds *public*" is a fraught, fragile project. For those of us studying places that we also call "home," these conversations may produce a profound sense of dislocation. To interrogate these intimacies and anxieties, we focus on three central questions: Why this place? What keeps us coming back? What role do we play in (re)producing narratives of inequality, uneven development, and global spectacles? In so doing, we seek to challenge dominant ways of touring, seeing, and knowing.

This book addresses these questions through the lens of Latin America and the Caribbean. As a new global economy transforms local life across the Global South, understanding a politics of return is central to the production of Latin America and the Caribbean as destination sites for tourism and as sites of intellectual production and nation building. We examine our complicity in producing global and local discourses that market Latin America and the Caribbean as places to be toured, experienced, and consumed. How do we grapple with the powerful discursive practices that are used to rationalize and justify tourism and neocolonial policies in this region? Through our personal travails with the messiness of "being there," we reconsider the high stakes involved in the interplay of race, class, gender, and sexuality in the history and geopolitics of this region. The experiences recalled here take place during specific historical moments in Latin America and the Caribbean. One of these formative moments is the 1990s, when this region was at the brink of economic globalization, in the throes of implementing neoliberal policies, and in the midst of recovering from decades-long civil wars. By the 2000s, new technologies relegated communicating via collect calls, pay phones, and air mail to a thing of the past, and they made it easier for us to maintain contact with interlocutors at our field sites. Hope—for a new economy, for a new era of political governance, for greater inclusion and recognition of Indigenous autonomy, for national reconciliation in the aftermath of war—abounded, even as resource extraction, austerity policies, debt escalation, political repression, and gender violence were ongoing. Several essays bear witness to the lived reality of these transformations. The essays that engage with the following decade—the 2010s—continue to ponder these changes, especially in the face of global economic crises. Our analyses benefit from a hindsight that comes with a long-term commitment to this region and the wisdom and consultation with a wide social network in Latin America and the Caribbean.

This book focuses on the travel experiences of scholars and journalists. James Clifford (1997, 6–7) describes traveling as "diverse practices of crossing, tactics of translation, experiences of double or multiple attachments" that are relationally constituted through "historical processes of displacement." Tourists, migrants, refugees, and ethnographers experience a sense of dislocation as they cross borders, go into exile, and make their way in another language, culture, and place. This book relies on Clifford's capacious definition of travel to bridge the similar yet divergent means by which scholars and journalists engage with their field sites and interlocutors, and to acknowledge that playing tourist often forms a central part of this engagement. Traveler, tourist, scholar, and journalist are not fixed identities and can be at play in different moments and places. The journalists included in this volume both earned doctoral degrees and currently work or previously worked in the academy, further muddying the divide between scholar and journalist. Nonetheless, we do not wish to assume a false equivalence, especially since these professions diverge in orientation, content, and politics. Instead, we see parallels in our roles as public intellectuals who seek to question, challenge, and disrupt "traveling" and "touring" in a region commonly referenced as part of the Global South.

Why This Place?

As scholars of Latin America and the Caribbean, we are frequently asked to serve as tour guides to popular tourist destinations in this region. "What country should I visit if I'm looking for an authentic Latin America?" a friend once asked. *Authentic*—along with *revolutionary*, *Indigenous*, and *underdeveloped*—is one of the adjectives used to render this region as ahistorical or fixed in time. Not surprisingly, nations rely on these tropes to fuel tourism economies. For example, favelas in Brazil have become popular attractions for reality tours, showcasing misery, poverty, and suffering (Freire-Medeiros 2009). Cuba and Nicaragua have successfully transformed their revolutionary sites and propaganda into compelling tourist attractions (Babb 2011). Likewise, the Mexican government selected the Yucatán Peninsula as an ideal location to build the international tourist center of Cancún because of its lush, "untouched" spaces, overabundance of Mayan archaeological sites, and cheap Indigenous labor (Castellanos 2010). The contributors to this volume take narratives of underdevelopment, revolution, and authenticity as starting points for a discussion of our involvement with Latin America and the Caribbean. For many of us, our initial forays and returns to this region were indeed inspired by revolutionary movements and personal quests to experience an imagined homeland. As such we are cognizant of the power and attraction of these master narratives. These tropes become signposts that mask contested histories and struggles over land, belonging, and Indigenous rights.

Walter Mignolo reminds us that Latin America is an invention rooted in empire and sustained by modernity. "To excavate the 'idea of Latin America,'" Mignolo (2005, xiii) suggests, "is, really, to understand how the West was born and how the modern world order was founded." By hailing the geopolitical formations and imperial fantasies that have produced "Latin America and the Caribbean," we acknowledge that what we write about this region plays a role in maintaining and contesting this fiction. Following Mignolo, we begin by acknowledging that this region is a geopolitical construct built out of a legacy of (neo)colonialism, Indigenous genocide, and slavery. Ultimately, we consider how these narratives shape how we think, talk, and write about this region, including our efforts to debunk them.

More recently, travel and tourism have become the bedrocks of Latin American and Caribbean economies as modern travel and mass tourism accelerated after World War II.[2] As the largest service sector industry in the world, travel and tourism contribute 9.8 percent (7.2 trillion U.S. dollars) of the global GDP. In Latin America, travel and tourism generate 3.4 percent of the GDP (WTTC 2015). The annual visitors include thousands of Western students funneled throughout the region to participate in "cross-cultural" exchanges. At the University of Minnesota, where I teach, study abroad is being promoted as a core undergraduate experience. Yet these types of scholastic exchanges may reproduce ahistorical, stereotypical notions of cultural authenticity and thus produce essentialized visions of life in Latin America and the Caribbean (e.g., Bruner 2005; Freire-Medeiros 2009). Scholars and journalists who travel throughout this region form part of this billion-dollar industry. As we travel in search of a news story or a new ethnographic perspective, we have become tourists (see Flores Martos and Ulysse in this volume). Occasionally we have led student exchange programs and participated in educational tours (see Behar and Moodie and Binford in this volume). Just as tourism has come increasingly under critical scrutiny (Desmond 1999; Urry 1990), Florence Babb (2011, 5–6) suggests that tourism encounters "warrant a closer examination . . . to recognize power and difference." The contributors explore these encounters to highlight the lessons learned from wielding our privilege and power in this region.

How (Not) to Reproduce Empire?

This book urges readers to gaze beyond popular frames of underdevelopment and political instability. In so doing, our goal is not to dismiss the very real impact of poverty and violence on marginalized and Indigenous communities. Instead through a focus on our personal experiences within systems of power and privilege, the book underscores the complexity of race relations, ethnic politics, and struggles for justice. By offering new narratives that challenge legacies of empire, it aims to disrupt hegemonic readings of Latin America and the Caribbean. It also endeavors to chip away at the ossified hierarchies of race, class, and gender perpetuated by the media and popular culture. Yet "being there" means contemplating race, class, and gender in relation to our multiple positionalities as scholars, as Westerners, as tourists, and—for some of us—as natives.

This volume builds on a tradition of critical reflection concerning travel, tourism, and ethnography.[3] It heeds the need to be vigilant of the epistemologies behind our methods and practices and of the errors that these conditions may inevitably produce (Bourdieu, Chamboredon, and Passeron 1991). In *Writing Culture*, James Clifford and George E. Marcus (1986) unveiled fieldwork as more than scientific inquiry, as centered on the production of text and the invention of culture. Following the reflexive turn in anthropology, Clifford and Marcus advanced the idea that "the poetic and the political are inseparable" (2).[4] In *Women Writing Culture*, Ruth Behar and Deborah A. Gordon (1996) provided a much-needed feminist corrective to a poetics that excluded women (and women of color) anthropologists whose innovative texts already embraced the notion that the personal is political. The ongoing debate about how to write about peoples and their cultures and who can claim authority is central to this project. Writing ethnography is inherently political; as a gendered, embodied, and affective practice, our engagement is central to this undertaking. By highlighting our autobiographies, our essays situate writing as taking place not only in the field but also in offices at universities, on tables in coffee shops, at desks in our bedrooms (where I sit now as I write), in places as distant as the United States and Europe.

This book is influenced by the lyrical works of anthropologists Ruth Behar (1996, 2013), Zora Neale Hurston (1935), and Renato Rosaldo (1993), who illustrate how joy, tragedy, and personal foibles can augment our understanding of the cultural import of daily life. Rosaldo (1993, 8) shrewdly reminds us that "all interpretations are provisional; they are made by positioned subjects who are prepared to know certain things and not others." Perspectives of social phenomena are always partial and dependent on the scale selected to magnify their scope and complexity (Strathern 2004). As positioned subjects, the contributors consider the limited nature of their perspectives. Even who they are when they travel is often subject to change. For example, during my first trip to Mexico's Yucatán Peninsula, I was shocked when Maya children called me a *gringa*. It was not a compliment, but an aspersion that was hurled at me when I walked around town as they rode past on their bikes. This term called attention to my privilege as an American. I was a foreigner, a *gringa*. In my experience as a Mexican immigrant growing up in California, this word was reserved for Anglos and was not synonymous with my Brown body. It took me weeks to stop cringing at this reminder of my difference. Our lived experiences inform our ways of seeing, knowing, and being, especially when we travel and conduct field research. These partial perspectives can lead us to make assumptions rooted in arrogance, misplaced empathy, and sheer outrage. Questioning this privilege entails reckoning with the systemic facets of poverty, race, and class in countries like Mexico and Brazil (see Castellanos and Klein this volume).

Despite the recent push to write "vulnerably," great skill is needed to balance autobiography with traditional ethnography and reporting (Behar 1996, 2013). While we may be plagued by doubt and misgivings, these insecurities are almost always absent from the written page. The essays by Behar, Flores, and Klein disclose these vulnerabilities and their effect on transforming the authors' relationships with students, interlocutors, and field sites. Not surprisingly, gender and sexuality are defining experiences in the field. They determine our access (or lack of it) to people, places, and spaces, especially as we move across gender systems. For women, women of color, and queer scholars, negotiating structured inequalities is a fraught process that can backfire and place us in harm's way (see Kastelein in this volume). We must learn to negotiate and subvert heteronormative and patriarchal norms that aim to contain our sensuality and physical mobility and to hinder our ways of seeing and knowing. Just as challenging, at times, is writing about "messy, subjective and intimate corporeal bodily processes" (Frohlick 2010, 52). Susan Frohlick observes that the ethnographer's experience has been "reduced largely to gazing." Our own bodies and the emotions and desires that they elicit are rarely theorized (Davies and Spencer 2010). For Vernadette Vicuña Gonzalez (2013, 2, 3), understanding the "regimes of feeling" that structure touring and traveling is essential to unmasking relations of power and the "traumas of cultural collision." Fear, violence, and pleasure are persistent, yet often ignored, undercurrents of the fieldwork experience (Nordstrom and Robben 1995; Rabinow 1977; Scheper-Hughes 1992). In his essay, Flores corrects this omission by centering the emotions—desire and guilt—that form part of ethnographic encounters, especially during moments of duress. Before leaving for the field, we are regaled with stories of romantic assignations, but we are also warned of tragic deaths. Carolyn Nordstrom and Antonius C. G. M. Robben (1995, 18) point out that we "are not immune from the violence that seems endemic to human society. Anthropologists have been assassinated, at home and in the field. They have been mugged, robbed, and raped." Our field sites include former war zones and current drug trafficking corridors (see Moodie and Binford in this volume). As such, we must learn to maneuver danger zones at great personal cost.

Half the contributors to this volume (Behar, Castellanos, Rocha, and Ulysse) were born and raised—during their childhood and/or into adulthood—in Latin America and the Caribbean and have immediate or extended families who continue to live in this region. Living in diaspora has strengthened our ties to this region, but it also produces tensions. For example, national politics are racialized in ways that those of us raised abroad may find troubling and challenging to understand. Indeed, a confrontation with the ugly side of racism is difficult to disentangle from the Brownness or Blackness of our own bodies. In Mexico, people assume that I am Indigenous because of the way that I look and the people with whom I spend my time. As a result, I have witnessed humiliating, racist treatment (intentional and otherwise) against Indigenous friends and colleagues. In becoming scholars and journalists, we are able to cultivate a level of privilege afforded to elites, predicated on gender, class, and/ or racial hierarchies, regardless of a lack of personal wealth or humble origins. Understanding these unequal but dependent relationships is no easy feat, especially when as American or European trained scholars we become elites upon crossing international borders. Class differences further compound this sense of dislocation. For example, maids can be found in elite to lower-middle-class households. They have established relationships with their employers that go beyond (in)formal contracts and that are solidified through ties of *compadrazgo* (godparents), patron-client relations, and/or abusive behavior. These relationships become even muddier when we shift our lens to families that are only marginally better off than their employees. When we hire domestic help in the field, Klein (in this volume) shows, we become complicit in sustaining racial and class hierarchies, regardless of any personal investment in dismantling these hierarchies.

Speaking from the intersections of race, class, and gender, this book asks us to reconsider our travel and returns to Latin America and the Caribbean as rooted in privilege, difference, and even nostalgia. It maps our efforts to examine how our idea(s) of Latin America have shifted over time and have shaped the people that we have become as writers, teachers, and activists. This book, in a sense, is our accounting of how to negotiate and resist reproducing empire.

From Initial Encounters to Alternative Contacts

In the first part of the book, we reflect on the dilemmas that arose during our initial travel experiences as researchers, writers, and tourists. Florence Babb (2011, 5) observes that too often the tourist encounter calls to mind the privilege of the Western traveler and the lack of agency of those being toured in the

Global South. To move beyond this vision of privilege and disadvantage, she proposes the "trope of the encounter precisely because it foregrounds the intimate relationship of those coming together from different cultures and societies *and* it does not already assume the outcome of any given engagement, granting agency to players who may be historically disadvantaged on the global stage" (emphasis added). Tourist encounters are critical in shaping the stories that we tell, but our research also includes getting to know local leaders, Indigenous communities, and government officials to create lasting friendships, professional alliances, and in some cases romantic relationships. To open up possibilities for reimagining and exploding binaries of the colonizer/colonized, academic/informant, and journalist/activist that acknowledge these deep social bonds, I reframe these encounters as moments of *alternative contact* (Lai and Smith 2010). Building on Gloria Anzaldúa's *borderlands* and Mary Louise Pratt's *contact zones*, Paul Lai and Lindsey Clair Smith (2010, 408) explain that a focus on alternative contact "foregrounds encounters as discrete sites of critical exchange that raise questions of ethical relations" and is attentive to asymmetric power relations. Examining the conjuncture of ethnography with empire and a history of academic training and advancement demands that we "think more concertedly about [our] methodological and political investments" (Lai and Smith 2010, 412). The contributors in this section thus interrogate their tourist and travel encounters in light of this asymmetry.

Anthropologist Misha Klein examines the privilege of perspective that she gained through living in Brazil. She initially traveled to Brazil to meet her fiancé's family and to look for a new dissertation research site. In the end, she spent over five years in Brazil. Klein describes this period as her "disappeared" years because it was marked by a profound sense of dislocation. She felt isolated from the person she had been prior to arriving in Brazil, a confident woman and scholar with close family ties. The person she became during that period struggled to stay connected and make sense of Brazil's social and economic disparities. As a "white" American woman, she also experienced great privilege in a society bound by rigid social hierarchies predicated on skin color and class. For Klein, "passing" across these fault lines was instrumental in reshaping her thinking about the world(s) that we inhabit and her place—as a citizen, tourist, scholar—within them.

Recounting his personal experiences working in Mexico and Bolivia, anthropologist Juan Antonio Flores Martos shares some of his most difficult, uncomfortable moments. Flores points out that ethnographic inquiry can often lead to highly anxious situations, although this problem is rarely made explicit in academic publications. For example, locals may heavily interrogate researchers, demanding to know their "real" motivations. This lack of trust can lead to feelings of fear, distrust, and guilt. For Flores, these emotions can manifest themselves in dreams, even nightmares, wherein the traveling academic is cast adrift in an unfamiliar world.

Journalist Barbara Kastelein shares the many personal and cultural negotiations required of an independent, Anglo female writer researching a book on the traditionally male world of the Acapulco cliff divers. After nearly a century as a tourist resort in a state plagued by violence and poverty, Acapulco is a city that plays host with a disconcerting blend of enthusiasm and cynicism. Yet Kastelein speaks of what lies beyond the pleasantries of a superficial greeting: of actual power relationships in the town, the double-meaning words and mind games, the possibility for slurred reputations, and the threat of blackmail. Kastelein mixes her own reportage with interviews with Acapulco inhabitants on the subject of outsiders to offer a disconcerting testimony on the intimate politics of gender, collegiality, and friendship. She illustrates how tension animates much of tourist relations.

Returns

According to art critic John Berger (1972, 7, 9), "the relation between what we see and what we know is never settled . . . we are always looking at the relation between things and ourselves. Our vision is continually active, continually moving, continually holding things in a circle around itself, constituting what is present to us as we are." Berger was writing about art, but the act of seeking an understanding of what we see and how we interpret it speaks to the contributors' efforts to make sense of the people and places they visit and come to think they know. As scholars and journalists of Latin America and the Caribbean, we have spent decades traveling and writing about this region. We have built successful, lucrative careers on these returns. Like Wilentz, we consider it crucial to assess the nature of these returns, the moments of discomfort, the vexing encounters. We interrogate our first forays into the field and our continual returns. How do these returns shape our understanding of ourselves and the people we study? How are these returns gendered, classed, and racialized? What lessons can be learned from a critical reflection of our initial and ongoing negotiations in the field? Writer Jamaica Kincaid (1988, 19) suggests that "every native of every place is a potential tourist, and every tourist is a native of somewhere." How might things be different if we were the ones being *toured*? Cognizant of these power differentials, essays in this section rethink the often rosy, conventional discussions of tourism, travel, and culture. Instead, we try to make sense of our own weariness and the pleasures, the discomfort, and the ugliness that we see—as we move between countries and languages in order to render visible this jarring sense of dislocation.

When anthropologist Ruth Behar was five years old, her family fled Cuba in protest against the Castro government. Unlike her parents, Behar is part of a generation of Cubans and Cuban Americans who today wish to build bridges with Cuba. Traveling to the island with a group of students in tow, Behar reflects on the process of bridge building and on the multiple risks involved in taking students abroad. When her students face a health scare, the responsibility of taking care of them weighs heavily on her. In her students' eschewal of the Cuba she knows well—a modern nation-state struggling with the baggage of a revolutionary history and Cold War geopolitics in the era of digital media and telecommunications—and desire for an authentic Cuba, a revolutionary Cuba that no longer exists, she sees her own reflection and that of Cuban Americans who came of age in the 1970s.

In my essay, I think through Cancún as more than just a tourist site, prompted by my experience with long-term fieldwork and by my position as a native, foreigner, tourist, and ethnographer. Marked as a foreigner and a native while doing research in Mexico, I was able to experience the "three faces" of Cancún: its hotel zone, middle-class center, and poor shantytowns. Reading beneath the surface of Mexican politics and class and ethnic differences, I suggest, demands that we look beyond an analogy of difference to think about the possibilities for connections as people traverse these zones daily. These crossings may be marked and destabilized by mobile bodies, but they continue to be embedded in historical shifts—both recent and long-standing—born by political, gender, ethnic, and class transformations. Cancún represents a Mexico that is in a state of constant transition even as it is deeply rooted in (neo)colonial histories of exploitation and privilege. These (dis)connections are visible from the moment tourists arrive in Cancún. As they are shuttled from the airport to their hotel in an air-conditioned taxi or van, tourists are inundated with images of Cancún as alluring, tropical, and modern. Yet the first question they ask destabilizes this image: is it safe to drink the water? This simple query encapsulates a colonial history of racial hierarchies and suspicion that continue to dominate how the Global South is read and imagined.

Feminist theorist Gloria Anzaldúa (1987) proclaimed that borders are open wounds that continuously grate and bleed as people cross from north to south and south to north. Anthropologists Ellen Moodie and Leigh Binford examine this wound through a look at solidarity tourism in El Salvador. They take us on a journey to the hamlet of El Mozote in northeastern El Salvador—tragically, the site of the largest massacre in the bloody Salvadoran Civil War (1979–92). On December 11, 1981, the Salvadoran Army raped, strangled, shot, and then burned the corpses of more than eight hundred civilians (largely women, children, and old men) in a vain attempt to root out antigovernment, leftist guerrillas. Following in the footsteps of hundreds of foreign delegations who have come to El Salvador in more recent years, Moodie and Binford travel to El Mozote. They examine the history and testimony of El Mozote survivors as part of what they term the *economy of pain* engendered in the making of solidarity/human rights/heritage tourism at the site. They suggest that this exchange between Salvadoran hosts and international guests often leads to simplified, exoticized historical narratives that are largely the result of foreign demand. Here, "tourists [tend to] seek out blood, death, and destruction, [as] guides and others feed these desires by portraying events in gruesome detail." As Moodie and Binford assert, local determination of an appropriate accounting of El Mozote has become a challenging affair when faced with the "enchanted internationalism" of enthusiastic travelers to this site.

Literary scholar Fernando de Sousa Rocha observes, "One is never more at home than as a tourist; one never achieves a higher sense of the familiar than as a foreigner." For Rocha, being a tourist in one's hometown—in his case, Rio de Janeiro, Brazil—involves failing to see the familiar. To upend this, he relies on the tourist strategies of "recording, storing, and remembering" as he guides us through Rio's monuments and *ruas* (streets). Interweaving his own memories with local practices of inhabiting these spaces, Rocha calls forth new interpretations of how these spaces are inhabited: by both city residents and visiting tourists. For Rocha, a process of making the familiar unfamiliar entails revisiting his own past—as a young child and a young man—and then considering these perspectives as seen by the person he is today. Through a "tour" of Rio, Rocha renders himself a "historical being" as he contrasts memory, landscape, and tourist experiences over time.

(De)Tours

I return to Haiti once more. This book closes with a poem about Haiti and Cuba by anthropologist Gina Athena Ulysse. During her first trip to Cuba, Ulysse was appalled by how the marketing of Blackness embedded in revolutionary narratives failed to engage with the continued oppression of Black people in contemporary Cuba. She observed that tourist performances marked a hypersexual Blackness as central to Cuba's identity: Black bodies dancing, Black folks revolting. Ulysse sees similarities between Cuba and her native homeland of Haiti, where successful revolutions did not translate into economic success for most Black people. They continue to congregate at the bottom, working menial jobs and performing minstrelsy. Ulysse's poem therefore challenges the global consumption of Blackness by calling forth a self that acknowledges this painful history and embraces her Blackness as it is, not as it is performed. For Ulysse (2015, xvii), Haiti has become her "point of departure, not [her] point of arrival."

A politics of return offers a contrapuntal perspective that recenters Latin America and the Caribbean as a starting point, a point of departure. Edward Said (1993) encouraged a *contrapuntal perspective* to undo the work of imperialism and grant complex personhood to the subaltern. Such an approach makes it possible to imagine a politics of return that pushes against linear mobility and binary thinking, to imagine cultural formations as circular, even zigzag, motions. Producing new narratives of Haiti that eschew simplistic explanations and stereotypes requires a fundamental shift in perspective (Ulysse 2015). Haiti, then, is no longer a spectacle but instead becomes a lens through which we read, filter, and imagine the world (Ulysse 2015; Wilentz 2013). Through contrapuntal readings, this book's contributors offer new departures, new (de)tours for decentering the West and disrupting the linearization of travel, theory, and social typologies (Coronil 1995; Lelièvre and Marshall 2015). In so doing, we unmask the politics of looking, the politics of knowledge production, the politics of spectacles and consumption, and the politics of empire. We hope that our reflections will help readers, as they forge their own touristic, scholastic, and political praxis, to think through their own power and privilege and thus encourage new conditions of possibility across geographies divided by race, class, gender, violence, and war.

Notes

1. Wilentz's initial interest in Haiti derived from her fascination with the Tonton Macoute militia, which terrorized the country during President Francois "Papa Doc" Duvalier's dictatorship (1957–71). She subsequently built a thriving career as a journalist and scholar by returning again and again to Haiti.
2. For a history of tourism, see Cormack 1998; Weiss 2004. For an overview of tourism studies, see Chambers 2010; Nash 1996; Smith 1977.
3. See Babb 2011; Behar 2013; Bruner 2005; Crapanzano 2015; Frohlick 2010; Geertz 1989, 1996; Harrison 2003, 2013; MacCannell 1999.
4. Works such as Elenore Smith Bowen's *A Return to Laughter* (1964) and Paul Rabinow's *Reflections on Fieldwork in Morocco* (1977) paved the way for reflexive ethnography.

References

Anzaldúa, Gloria. 1987. *Borderlands/Las Fronteras: The New Mestiza.* San Francisco: Aunt Lute Books.

Babb, Florence. 2011. *The Tourism Encounter: Fashioning Latin American Nations and Histories.* Stanford, Calif.: Stanford University Press.

Behar, Ruth. 1996. *The Vulnerable Observer: Anthropology That Breaks Your Heart.* Boston: Beacon Press.

Behar, Ruth. 2013. *Traveling Heavy: A Memoir in Between Journeys.* Durham, N.C.: Duke University Press.

Behar, Ruth, and Deborah A. Gordon, eds. 1996. *Women Writing Culture.* Berkeley: University of California Press.

Berger, John. 1972. *Ways of Seeing.* New York: Penguin Books.

Bourdieu, Pierre, et al. 1999. *The Weight of the World: Social Suffering in Contemporary Society.* Translated by Priscilla Parkhurst Ferguson. Stanford, Calif.: Stanford University Press.

Bourdieu, Pierre, Jean-Claude Chamboredon, and Jean-Claude Passeron. 1991. *The Craft of Sociology: Epistemological Preliminaries.* Edited by Beate Krais. Translated by Richard Nice. Berlin: Walter de Gruyter.

Bowen, Elenore Smith. 1964. *A Return to Laughter: An Anthropological Novel.* New York: Random House.

Bruner, Edward. 2005. *Culture on Tour: Ethnographies of Travel.* Chicago: University of Chicago Press.

Castellanos, M. Bianet. 2010. *A Return to Servitude: Maya Migration and the Tourist Trade in Cancún.* Minneapolis: University of Minnesota Press.

Chambers, Erve. 2010. *Native Tours: The Anthropology of Travel and Tourism.* Long Grove: Waveland Press.

Clifford, James. 1997. *Routes.* Cambridge, Mass.: Harvard University Press.

Clifford, James, and George E. Marcus, eds. 1986. *Writing Culture: The Poetics and Politics of Ethnography.* Berkeley: University of California Press.

Cormack, Bill. 1998. *A History of Holidays, 1812–1990.* London: Routledge.

Coronil, Fernando. 1995. "Introduction to the Duke University Press Edition." In *Cuban Counterpoint*, by Fernando Ortiz, ix–lvi. Durham, N.C.: Duke University Press.

Crapanzano, Vincent. 2015. *Recapitulations.* New York: Other Press.

Davies, James, and Dimitrina Spencer, eds. 2010. *Emotions in the Field: The Psychology and Anthropology of Fieldwork Experience.* Stanford, Calif.: Stanford University Press.

Desmond, Jane C. 1999. *Staging Tourism: Bodies on Display from Waikiki to Sea World.* Chicago: University of Chicago Press.

Freire-Medeiros, Bianca. 2009. "The Favela and Its Touristic Transits." *Geoforum* 40: 580–88.

Frohlick, Susan. 2010. "The Sex of Tourism? Bodies Under Suspicion in Paradise." In *Thinking Through Tourism*, edited by Julie Scott and Tom Selwyn, 51–70. Oxford: Berg.

Geertz, Clifford. 1989. *Works and Lives: The Anthropologist as Author.* Stanford, Calif.: Stanford University Press.

Geertz, Clifford. 1996. *After the Fact: Two Countries, Four Decades, One Anthropologist.* Cambridge: Harvard University Press.

Harrison, Julia. 2003. *Being a Tourist: Finding Meaning in Pleasure Travel.* Vancouver: University of British Columbia Press.

Harrison, Julia. 2013. *A Timeless Place: The Ontario Cottage.* Vancouver: University of British Columbia Press.

Hurston, Zora Neale. 1935. *Mules and Men.* New York: HarperCollins.

Kincaid, Jamaica. 1988. *A Small Place.* New York: Farrar, Straus and Giroux.

Lai, Paul, and Lindsey Claire Smith. 2010. "Introduction." *American Quarterly* 62 (3): 407–36.

Lelièvre, Michelle A., and Maureen E. Marshall. 2015. "'Because life it selfe is but motion': Toward an Anthropology of Mobility." *Anthropological Theory* 15 (4): 434–71.

MacCannell, Dean. 1999. *The Tourist: A New Theory of the Leisure Class.* Berkeley: University of California Press.

Mignolo, Walter. 2005. *The Idea of Latin America.* Malden, Mass.: Blackwell.

Nash, Dennison. 1996. *The Anthropology of Tourism.* Bingley, UK: Emerald Group.

Nordstrom, Carolyn, and Antonius C. G. M. Robben, eds. 1995. *Fieldwork Under Fire: Contemporary Studies of Violence and Survival.* Berkeley: University of California Press.

Rabinow, Paul. 1977. *Reflections on Fieldwork in Morocco.* Berkeley: University of California Press.

Rosaldo, Renato. 1993. *Culture and Truth: The Remaking of Social Analysis.* Boston: Beacon Press.

Said, Edward W. 1993. *Culture and Imperialism*. New York: Alfred A. Knopf.

Schepher-Hughes, Nancy. 1992. *Death Without Weeping: The Violence of Everyday Life in Brazil*. Berkeley: University of California Press.

Smith, Valene. 1977. *Hosts and Guests: The Anthropology of Tourism*. Philadelphia: University of Pennsylvania.

Strathern, Marilyn. 2004. *Partial Connections*. Walnut Creek, Calif.: AltaMira Press.

Ulysse, Gina Athena. 2015. *Why Haiti Needs New Narratives: A Post-Quake Chronicle*. Middletown, Conn.: Wesleyan University Press.

Urry, John. 1990. *The Tourist Gaze: Leisure and Travel in Contemporary Societies*. London: Sage.

Vicuña Gonzalez, Vernadette. 2013. *Securing Paradise: Tourism and Militarism in Hawai'i and the Philippines*. Durham, N.C.: Duke University Press.

Weiss, Thomas. 2004. "Tourism in America Before World War II." *Journal of Economic History* 64 (2): 289–327.

Wilentz, Amy. 2013. *Farewell, Fred Voodoo: A Letter to Haiti*. New York: Simon and Schuster.

WTTC (World Travel and Tourism Council). 2015. *Travel and Tourism: Economic Impact 2015 Latin America*. London: WTTC.

PART I

Encounters

ONE

Privileges of the First World

Reflections on Another Life in Brazil

MISHA KLEIN

Exiles

I had not planned to stay in Brazil. Until a few months earlier, I had not planned to go to Brazil at all. Then, my plan was just to go meet my fiancé's family before doing ethnographic fieldwork in Guatemala for my doctoral dissertation in anthropology at UC Berkeley. I had already conducted summer research in a multicultural community on the Caribbean coast of Guatemala and presented on this research at an international Caribbean studies conference. Rather than the troubled national politics of Guatemala, it was academic politics that forced me to abandon that project. The momentum knocked out of me, I foundered. With a round-trip ticket to Brazil in hand, and no dissertation project, I went to Brazil with the intention of using the visit to see whether I could come up with a new research idea. The decision was one of necessity, so I read some ethnography and fiction about Brazil, and I figured that my Spanish would get me through in the short term.

In the initial months, I described my experiences to family and friends in long, detailed letters, complete with explanatory footnotes. Then, without meaning to, I vanished. It was not a political disappearance but an existential one. I entered into a kind of self-exile. The person I was before going to Brazil became subsumed by the life I was living. I was not fully aware of it, except in the pangs of homesickness, of *saudades*, that distinctive Portuguese word for longing and nostalgia and bittersweet remembrances (DaMatta 1993), *saudades* made more intense by writing. It was simply too difficult to live in one place and think about another. Later, when an acquaintance in the small Brazilian city where I lived made an offhand remark about how well she knew me, I retorted with a little too much vehemence that she did not know me, because none of the things and none of the people that made me who I was existed there. It was a sudden insight into how identities are formed in relation to others and how our sense of self derives in part from the way that we are reflected in others' eyes. Indeed, I felt as if I was living someone else's life, and I—the person I was before Brazil—had ceased to exist. I do not mean this in the romantic way that foreigners so often talk about the transformative effect that Brazil has on them. I mean it in a pragmatic sense, having to do with social relations and day-to-day existence, but also, ultimately, in the sense of occupying a different place in the world.

I was one of a handful of long-term foreign residents in São Carlos do Pinhal, a small city in "the interior" (inland) of the state of São Paulo. There were South Americans from several bordering nations who usually spoke a blend of Portuguese and Spanish known as "Portunhol" (*português* + *espanhol*) as well as some multigenerational Japanese families whose Japan-born elders never learned Portuguese.[1] There were also Brits, Russians, Germans, and Hungarians, mostly associated with the two universities in town or the English school with the "British English" marketing niche that glorified Britain's colonial history in its advertising: "Learn English with the ones who taught English to the world!" They might as well have promoted their school by inviting Brazilians to come learn English from the ones who started Brazil down the path of destructive national debt[2]—or the ones most experienced at crushing heritage languages.

One key difference between my formative experiences living in the interior of São Paulo and the experiences of cultural tourists who seek "authentic" cross-cultural encounters (Babb 2012) is that I ended up in a region that did not offer evident cultural difference or regional folkloric traditions, such as the gaucho culture of the South or the many artistic and musical traditions of the Northeast. Quite the opposite. On my first walk around town I saw graffiti spray-painted on a wall ordering "nordestinos fora" (northeasterners out), expressing a regional bigotry and rejection of the folkloric that I later came to understand as loaded with racial and class biases. Rather than being in a place with a touristic draw, I was in what Julia Harrison (2003, 171) calls a *black hole*, a place not worth knowing or visiting, at least not according to the usual touristic criteria: the interior of São Paulo was not exotic.

My experiences would have been entirely different had I lived in one of the country's cosmopolitan metropolises, like Rio de Janeiro or the city of São Paulo. Had I been in a big city, in a more touristed, multicultural environment, surrounded by other English speakers, I would have experienced less cultural isolation. Instead, I was fully immersed in a provincial town inhabited predominantly by practicing Roman Catholics (or *católico, apostólico, romano,* as the devout say).[3] The town was in an agricultural area that had been transformed by industrial-scale monocropping, first by the coffee boom at the end of the nineteenth century, then by oranges, and then by sugarcane to support the production of ethanol that fueled over half the Brazilian fleet.[4] During the sugarcane harvests, the ash from the burned fields along with the long, curled ghosts of grassy leaves would rain down on the town, covering everything with a fine gray powder. While not without its own ethereal beauty, the ash contributed to chronic respiratory problems in the region.

What began as a visit turned into over five years without a trip "home," to the United States, to my family and friends, to my graduate program. When I returned to the United States, I stayed for less than a year, and then I went back to Brazil, this time to the state capital, the city of São Paulo, for fieldwork. I returned again to the United States to write my dissertation and complete my doctorate, and eventually I landed a job in the middle of farm country, again, this time in Oklahoma. Another black hole, another "fly-over" region, another place with deep red dirt.[5] These experiences marked me, transformed me by changing my perspective on the world and my place in it. They also changed my understanding of the United States, in part because compelling parallels exist between the United States and Brazil. However, though my experiences were personally difficult, they were inflected with multiple forms of privilege—race, class, citizenship—that facilitated my movement, contributed to my ability to blend in, colored my expectations of what life could bring, and ultimately afforded me choices, though I did not necessarily realize it at the time.

Lessons

I first set foot in Brazil at the very end of 1992, completely unprepared to understand the transformations that were already taking place in that country[6] and utterly ignorant of the ways that my life would be transformed the moment I stepped off the plane. I was already familiar with the sudden feeling of regret I experienced; I had stepped off of other planes (and trains) in other countries and similarly asked myself what I had done, and why, why, why had I not just stayed home where people and things were familiar and I spoke the language. Nevertheless, I sought out these opportunities—though never the most adventuresome ones, since they usually involved language study rather than mountain climbing—each one feeling like a leap into an abyss. This time, instead of standing in the airport in exhausted bewilderment, taking in the bustle and unfamiliar smells, and looking for anything that might indicate the direction of my next mode of transportation, I was swept into the arms of my fiancé and members of his large family, and next I knew we were in an oversized Ford truck on a multilane highway driving through a soft green landscape.[7] I had absolutely no idea in what direction we were headed, nor how long it would take to get there. Although I tried to be polite and engaged, after a twelve-hour overnight flight, I kept dozing and caught only glimpses of the countryside.

I was travel weary, sleep deprived, and resisting the feeling that I had made a terrible mistake; my disorientation was intensified by my lack of Portuguese. I spoke Spanish fairly fluently and had spent enough time in Mexico and Guatemala for their landscapes to become familiar, but Brazil was something else entirely. In fact, the landscape around me looked like central California and more familiar than any I had seen in my travels, except that I could not understand the signs, and what I could read caused my creeping anxiety to intensify. At fairly regular intervals along the road were shacks with hand-painted signs reading *borracharia*. In Spanish, *borracho* means "drunk," and the suffix *-aria* means "place of"—a pizzeria, for example, is a place to get pizza. So, assuming that *borracho* was a cognate in Spanish and Portuguese, I thought that the signs advertised places to get drunk, and I was tremendously uncomfortable by how blatant these signs were, marking no-name drinking establishments along a major highway. My internal alarm fought silently with my cultivated sense of cultural relativism that reminded me to keep an open mind until I understood more—but I was unsure about this encouragement of drinking and driving. I knew that there was overlap between Spanish and Portuguese but did not know at the time that there were many false cognates. I later learned that in Portuguese *borracha* means "rubber," and that the shacks appropriately placed next to the road offered tire repair services. The story later became one that

I could add to rounds of tales of cross-cultural misunderstandings, a favorite social activity.[8] For anthropologists, such "mistakes" in the field are often key moments of insight, and the ability to laugh at one's own foibles is essential for making personal connections. What began as a misunderstanding became part of fitting in.

After about a three-hour drive, I arrived at the modest home of my new *sogra* (mother-in-law). In Brazil, affinal kinship terms are employed as soon as a relationship is deemed serious, and their use is a signal of social recognition. As I had traveled thousands of miles to be there, she was definitely my *sogra*. Although I did not know it ahead of time, it was in her house that I was to stay, and although I had not planned to do so and although I did not really want to do so, it was in her house that I remained for over five years.

As I expected, my Spanish provided a base from which to begin learning Portuguese, with the exception of those false cognates, but it soon gave way to a mostly monolingual Portuguese existence. Thanks to the exaggerated plots and repeating scenes of prime-time *novelas* (soap operas), which I watched along with everyone else, I quickly picked up Portuguese. With the help of an enthusiastic eleven-year-old niece, I learned Portuguese vocabulary; certain words still recall for me her rounded handwriting on the labels that we stuck on items all over her grandmother's house.

Not surprisingly, I had more to learn than the language. There were social mores (some Brazilian and some just the kind of small-town ways of interacting that were not part of my experience), and folk beliefs, and popular pastimes. There were little details of daily life, like electric showerheads and lizards in the bathroom, that had to do with where and how I was living and the resources at my disposal. All together they gave me a different perspective than I would have gained had I lived in a new high-rise apartment or in a big city, as I did later while doing fieldwork in the state's capital, São Paulo. At my first *carnaval*, I watched the draggy small-town parade, a sad suggestion of the glorious spectacles that take place in the big cities; I also watched the nationally broadcast coverage of those big parades on television and danced the night away at a local social club (the trick to staying energetic all night is to never sit down) and ate restorative soup at four in the morning. Though I had never been interested in car racing and had never even heard of Formula 1, I joined others around television sets to watch driver Ayrton Senna win race after race until his death in a horrible crash, and then I watched the nation mourn in a way that has no parallel in the United States, except perhaps following the assassination of

Kennedy. I watched *futebol*, especially the national soccer team, rejoiced in the streets when Brazil won the World Cup in 1994, and was dejected when it lost in the final game against France in 1998. I learned that the south of Brazil gets hit by cold fronts that can drop the temperature by forty degrees in an hour; indeed, I learned that however much Brazil is a "tropical country," as the song refrain goes, the south of that continent-sized country can get terribly cold.[9] Living practically on top of the Tropic of Capricorn, I experienced both the heat of the tropics and the cold of the temperate region to the south. In a home with neither air conditioning nor insulation, I experienced all these weather variations intensely, *na pele* (in the skin), as they say in Brazil.

Being a native English speaker was one of many privileges that gave me great advantage while living in Brazil. Whether teaching for one of the private schools or offering small-group or individual classes on my own, I immediately found that I had a marketable skill that was in demand. I also did translation and English editorial work for the professors and graduate students at the two major universities in town, one state and one federal. These scholars had to present and publish their work in English, even in conferences and journals in Brazil; while some balked at this linguistic colonialism, others were resigned to the dominance of English and submitted to the regime so that their contributions would be less likely to be ignored by the international scholarly community. I did cosmic penance for unknown crimes correcting minor grammatical errors and prepositions as the English editor for the *Journal of the Brazilian Chemical Society*, which publishes in English. Working for thoroughbred horse breeders, I translated documents for exporting horse semen. These and many other experiences during my time in Brazil were set apart from those available to tourists; while some tourist experience is embodied, the emphasis is overwhelmingly on the visual (Harrison 2003, 208; see also Bruner 2005). Ultimately, I had such varied experiences and learned so much not just because I was in another country but because I was integrated into social worlds that would have been equally unfamiliar in the United States. I did not go to Brazil primarily as a scholar and researcher, at least not initially, and so what I learned went well beyond anything I would have sought out or encountered on my own terms. However, I was already a doctoral candidate in anthropology before going to Brazil, so I was primed by my studies and a previous research project to notice certain things and ask certain questions. Those observations and insights eventually led to my formulating a new research project, one that was grounded in my experiences in Brazil.

Living off the tourist track in Brazil, I had to deal with a good many things that visitors rarely do, and so I learned about the minutia of ways around the system, especially when the system does not work (or does not work in the way that one would wish). I learned about the *jeitinho*, the little ways of getting around rules and other impediments (Barbosa 1995).[10] I learned how to balance a checkbook when inflation was nearly 50 percent a month.[11] I learned to keep my balance (in both senses) through multiple currency readjustments in which three zeroes were lopped off of 10,000, 50,000, and 100,000 bills, which were then renamed while we waited for new currency to be printed. I learned to drive (without a license) through red lights at night to avoid holdups because that was the *safe* thing to do. I learned to *live* there, and that meant learning to do what was needed to get by. In other words, I learned the *jeito brasileiro*, how to do things the Brazilian way, though this is less technique and more of an outlook.

(Dis)Encounters

I slid between known worlds and encountered things I had not anticipated in other ways as well. Prior to arriving in Brazil, I had been excited by the prospect of witnessing the political transformations that were underway. Following the country's two decades of repressive military rule and a successful transition to democratic governance, Brazilians had exercised their new rights to rally for the impeachment of the charismatic but corrupt Fernando Collor de Mello, the first democratically elected president in twenty-nine years. I arrived in Brazil the day before Collor's last day in office, and I expected to see more dancing in the streets.[12] Instead, I awoke on December 29, my first full day in Brazil, to find everyone crying. As it turned out, the demise of Collor was completely over-shadowed by the brutal murder of Daniella Perez, the beautiful young star of the popular prime-time *novela, Corpo e Alma (Body and Soul)*. The story unfolded in a way that paralleled the sorts of plot lines that grip the country six nights a week on prime time. Perez was stabbed to death by her costar Guilherme de Pádua and his wife, Paula Thomaz. While mourning her daughter and dealing with the press, Perez's mother, Glória Perez, who was also the screenwriter for the series, was then forced to account for the sudden disappearance of two principal char-acters, their actors—one dead and the other imprisoned—suddenly unavailable. What was baffling for me on that first morning in Brazil was the intensity of the emotion of those around me, as if people had lost someone close to them. One new sister-in-law finally explained that "if it could happen to her it could happen to anyone," a sentiment repeated whenever a wealthy or famous Brazilian suffered the assaults that are so familiar to the popular classes. I did not yet understand the special role that the high-production nighttime soap operas play in Brazilian social life, and I soon found it valuable to watch them in order to follow conversations in which *novela* characters were incorporated as easily as if they were friends and relatives. Through watching the *novelas*, I also developed a "flexible" ear for regional and class variations of Brazilian Portuguese (at least insofar as the Globo television network allowed such deviations from the southeastern coastal norm) because of the situated plot lines that ran for a few months before the stories resolved and a new *novela* began, set in another city or another epoch.[13]

The permeable line between reality and fiction, and especially between daily life and *novela*, was evident in more than the unfolding political drama or the tangle of the lives of *novela* characters and the actors who played them. This slippage between the tangible and the imagined is the basis for the literary genre known as *magical realism*, but this approach to writing is not merely a stylistic innovation; the scenes that color magical realist literature are plucked from everyday life. Rooted in Catholic mysticism and a Mediterranean propensity for magical thinking is a cultural ethos by which people do not seek to dismiss that which does not have a rational explanation but rather prefer to mull it over and explore the possibilities and improbabilities.

I was reminded of this porous barrier between fiction and nonfiction whenever I encountered Roma people (Gypsies), known as *ciganos* in Brazil. More than colorful characters populating the imagination of Southern Cone novelists, Roma live throughout the Americas, usually in a nomadic and socially (and often legally) peripheral existence. In Brazil, Roma are highly visible because of their distinctive style of dress and the way they often move in large groups, always on the margins. Once while having coffee in the center of São Carlos, I observed a somewhat disheveled Roma woman enter the establishment with her own cup, which she tapped lightly on the counter to request coffee. When she was ignored, she tapped it again more insistently, until she was gruffly served; she then paid, took her coffee, and left. She clearly expected to be unwelcome (so much so that she brought her own cup) and came prepared to insist on service. Without acknowledging that she had been mistreated, two men sitting at the counter loudly commented that they wished "our" *ciganas* were as beautiful as the ones on television. They were referring to the captivating group of Roma (played by non-Roma actresses) on the popular prime-time *novela*

Explode Coração, coincidentally written by Glória Perez, the screenwriter of *Corpo e Alma*.[14] The exotic television *ciganas* danced provocatively and smiled alluringly, without having to suffer the humiliations of poverty and prejudice.

These encounters can feel apocryphal, more like symbolically loaded dramatic scenes than quotidian encounters. However, I had enough of these moments to recognize them as part of the magical realism of the everyday. Although not all such moments involved Roma, their frequent invocations of the mystical made these moments especially charged. In one instance, I crossed paths with a Roma woman who appealed to the ubiquitous concept of *inveja* (envy). Having finally traded in a car that I really disliked (with doors so wide that they practically blocked the street when open) for a better used car, my new car was in an accident within an hour of the trade, and I was suddenly without a car at all. The following day I had an appointment on the other side of town, so I had to walk in the hot December sun, up one side of a steep hill, across the plaza at the top, and down the other side. In the very center of the plaza at the hill's summit, a Roma woman stepped into my path. Offering to read my palm, she told me that there was a lot of *inveja* interfering with my life. It was a cinematic moment, one that could have led to my agreeing to have my palm read so that she could reveal the source of the destructive envy that was troubling me (and was clearly the reason that the car got wrecked). I was late, so instead of giving in to the fantasy, I said "pois é" (so it is) and continued on my way.

The destructive power of envy and its conjoined twin, the evil eye, are widely accepted parts of public discourse. Bowls of salt and special plants (such as the tellingly named *lingua de sogra* [mother-in-law's tongue]) are strategically placed in homes and businesses to "absorb" envy, and I heard many accounts of how a designated plant took the hit for someone during a visit by an envious neighbor or relative, suddenly crumpling under the weight of her (always her) toxic jealousy. So widespread are these beliefs that a billboard for an insurance company on a major thoroughfare in the city of São Paulo declared, "We offer coverage for everything but the evil eye." Envy may be an acknowledged source of troubles, but the company cannot insure against it.

Disruptions

A number of factors contributed to my "disappearance." Some of these were rooted in my personal life and relationships back home, and some had to do with my having lost the rhythm of my graduate studies and my original doctoral research project in Guatemala. Certainly, a big part of my isolation was a symptom of being in a troubled relationship. However, bureaucratic, pragmatic, and even technological factors also contributed.

The technological issues were simple, the sorts of problems that would not occur today. When I first arrived in Brazil, there was no internet. I relied on "snail mail" to keep contact with family and friends, and I made extremely rare and very expensive phone calls to my mother. However, long delays occurred between letters, and some correspondence went missing or was returned as undeliverable (for reasons that were never made clear, since the addresses were correct). All of these factors made it difficult to maintain a flow of communication. The internet came to Brazil much later than it did to the United States, and it came to where I was in the interior even later. I still remember the first astonishing experience of a back-and-forth email correspondence with a colleague in the United States over a matter of hours, something that previously would have taken weeks or months. Today, with the ease of electronic communication, I would not have lost contact with my family and friends, or myself, and I probably would not have stayed so long. With the thickened bureaucracy and increase in surveillance that we are now subjected to, I probably would not have been able to stay.

The bureaucratic problems had to do with my legal status in the country. Originally intending to stay only briefly, I went to Brazil with a round-trip ticket and a three-month tourist visa that was renewable for another three months. However when I went to the state capital to renew the visa, what should have been a straightforward process turned into an all-day affair that required the deployment of personal connections and the greasing of palms. After that, I would have needed to leave the country to get another visa. But even a quick trip to neighboring Paraguay or Argentina required more money than I had, so six months turned into a year, then two, then three . . . and all the while I was living and working without legal documentation. In other words, I was "undocumented," an experience that is never far from my mind when I hear about the far more dehumanizing experiences of those far from home who are making a life in the United States (and Europe). I had not exactly *chosen* to migrate to Brazil (I was drawn by a relationship), nor had I precisely *chosen* to stay (I was stuck in a relationship), nor had I decided to willfully, abjectly flout the laws of the state (I was simply broke). Nevertheless, through a complex set of personal, affective, financial, bureaucratic, and geopolitical factors, I found myself living in Brazil for years without proper legal status, more of an outcome than a decision directly made. That same nexus of factors also made it difficult for me to extract myself from my situation.

During that time, my distressed mother would warn me not to let my passport expire. I knew the expiration date and dismissed her prods as annoyances, until the sickening day when I looked at my passport and realized that I had misremembered the expiration date, and it had passed a year before. So now not only did I not have proper documentation in Brazil but I was also without valid documents from my own country. I called the U.S. Consulate in São Paulo with tremendous trepidation, worried that I would be punished and would have to wait for months for my documentation to be rectified. Instead, I found that the U.S. government was utterly unconcerned with my status in Brazil or my passport's validity. As a U.S. citizen I did not need a valid passport to return home—though that was in the pre-9/11 days, and this lapse would likely never be permissible today (as seems to be the case with so many of the follies of my youth). All that I needed to renew my passport was a passport photo, my old passport, a standard fee, and an open phone line (again, preinternet) so that the consulate could contact the State Department and make sure I was not wanted by Interpol. With documentation in hand, I took the three-hour bus ride to São Paulo to renew my passport. The consulate closed for a long lunch break, making it imperative that I arrive early enough to be attended in the morning so that I would not have to wait until the afternoon and lose the entire day. Since I did not want to travel with cash for the fee, I planned on getting cash out of an ATM on the Avenida Paulista, known as "Brazil's Wall Street," just a few long, steep blocks from the consulate. As bad luck would have it, that morning the entire electronic banking system shut down, so I walked up and down the Avenida in search of a functioning ATM, and I ultimately had to wait for a bank branch to open (at 10 a.m., earlier than the "bankers' hours" observed in the interior). Cash in hand and thoroughly agitated, I grabbed a cab to race downhill, but I distracted the cabbie with my tale so that he drove past the consulate and had to go back around the block. Dashing to the consulate, expecting delays and disappointments, I was instead ushered in past a long line of Brazilians that stretched down the block and around the corner, past the high security at the entrance, and up the stairs. I presented my materials, answered a couple of questions, raised my hand and swore it was all true, and was back out on the sidewalk in about half an hour, dazed and blinking in the bright sunlight, but with my new passport in hand. The privilege of a U.S. passport has rarely been so obvious to me; I held in my hand a rather inexpensive document that allowed me ease of movement across international borders, an ease that I was entitled to by virtue of my place of birth. The hundreds of people still waiting in line, some of whom were being paid to wait in line for someone else, seeking permission to visit my country, would pay much more for much less. Although it was never my intent, the privilege of my citizenship allowed me to violate the laws of their country with impunity.

Privileges

I was able to live and work in Brazil without proper legal status and with minimal fear because of good linguistic skills, a bit of luck, and a number of intersecting social privileges. Having a facility for language, I quickly gained fluency in Portuguese and eventually could "pass" as Brazilian to the point that by the time I left I was asked for my Brazilian passport at the airport. After a few years, people told me that when they met me in the early days of my stay, when I still had an accent, they thought that either I had a slight speech impediment or I was from another region of the country; they could detect something different, but rarely did anyone pick up on an identifiable foreign accent. That was my cloak of invisibility.

Further, though I resist admitting it, however *emotionally* ungrounding those family relationships may have been, having a place to stay and being attached to a kin network also afforded me a kind of grounding that tourists rarely experience. I may not have *felt* that I belonged, because of the complicated and uncomfortable family dynamics, but I did have a place to belong, as even now the occasional message from a former niece or nephew reminds me.

Another factor that contributed to my cloak of invisibility had to do with where I fit in the Brazilian racial scheme. Being at the white end of the color spectrum meant that I was not subject to the suspicious gaze of the law or society at large: I did not draw attention. Whiteness operated in my favor in two intersecting ways. First was my own life experience of being "unmarked," which meant that I was unself-conscious; I had the privilege of not having to think, or strategize, or doubt. Second was the way that whiteness operates in Brazil, as an index of status. While this second point may seem obvious enough from the perspective of the U.S. racial/color scheme, whiteness carried other meanings in Brazil that reinforced what I knew intellectually about race as a social construct and not a biological reality. I already had experience elsewhere in the Caribbean and Latin America that showed me how fluid and truly social racial categorizations could be; on multiple occasions I had been assessed by strangers, acquaintances, and colleagues as belonging to an ill-defined mixed status on the dubious basis of the tannability of my skin (a trace of some Sephardic ancestry) or my ability to dance. In Brazil, where scholars have documented dozens of color terms to describe different combinations of physical features and social qualities (i.e., Harris 1964), whiteness can carry such social meanings as economic class and nationality as well as ethnicity and ancestry. People who knew I was from the United States and who were lighter skinned than me offered dire warnings about the intensity of the Brazilian sun. A dermatologist (of Japanese descent) recommended that I walk with a sun umbrella, to which I responded that I would consider it on the day that I saw his (white) wife and daughter with one. Although protecting my skin probably would have been a good idea, I repeatedly found that neither the shade of my skin nor even my ancestry prevailed in the way acquaintances interpreted my whiteness; some saw me as whiter by virtue of my nationality, a further example of how social factors enter into the calculus of race/color in Brazil.

Nationality figured into my social positioning in other ways too. The political and economic superiority of the United States stuck to me, however ill-deserved on my part or problematic on the part of the United States. Not only was I presumed to be at the far white end of the color spectrum (within a racial grammar that reads the United States as a "white" nation),[15] but also I was presumed to have greater economic power than I actually did; no matter how limited my financial resources, I could still break through class barriers that are far less permeable for most Brazilians. This, too, allowed me a certain invisibility or capacity to "pass" once my linguistic skills developed enough to no longer draw attention. Then there was the status of being from the United States, which simply meant that I had an access that was desirable, whether for the purposes of immigration, study, or travel—especially to places like Walt Disney World, where I have never been, to the shock of many middle-class Brazilians for whom Disney World is both a major tourist destination and a rite of passage (O'Dougherty 2002).

Being connected to a Brazilian family meant that I was integrated into a social world and did not have to figure everything out for myself. Having been raised middle class and with the expectation of the full rights of citizenship in the United States meant that I was confident in my movements, trusting that things would work as they should, eventually, and these expectations allowed me to carry on in the everyday as if I could continue to count on the unexamined privileges that I had enjoyed for most of my life. My economic privileges extended to being better prepared to ride the changes that came with the Plano Real, which was introduced in 1994 in an attempt to halt hyperinflation and stabilize the Brazilian economy through the introduction of international standards and neoliberal policies. I watched the confusion of people trying to calculate their change following the introduction of the new economic plan, people who did not have my experience of comparing the Brazilian currency to the dollar; as I observed confused transactions with cashiers, I worried about those with barely a grade-school education, and a weak one at that, the 60 percent of the population that was functionally illiterate. When I returned to Brazil to do fieldwork in 1999, I saw the new currency crash on the world market, doubling the price of anything that was tied to the U.S. dollar, from imported goods to imported labor. It also meant that my fieldwork expenses were cut nearly in half. By then, I no longer had a place and a family in Brazil, and I was once again a traveler, a researcher, a foreigner benefiting from a favorable exchange rate, another unearned advantage from global inequality.

Perhaps the most unexpected way in which my status as U.S. citizen influenced my social position in Brazil was how my course of study was interpreted by people I met. Not long after arriving in Brazil, I met a man in one of the lovely, tree-filled plazas onto which small store-front bars spilled out, laying claim to public space by placing small metal tables with beverage company logos for groups to gather around to cool off in the summer evenings over "stupidly cold" beer. I think that the man must have spoken English since I was still limping along in Portuguese, and I do not think that we ever met again. He was an engineer, probably associated with one of the universities in town; I no longer remember what sort of engineer, but I do know that I met more engineers in Brazil than ever before and found out that there are more kinds of engineers than I had ever imagined. (As an undergraduate, I used to study in the engineering library in college because I was assured of not knowing anyone.) When I told him that I was a graduate student in anthropology, he responded: "Ah, anthropology, privilege of the First World." I have mulled over this phrase many times in the years since this encounter and contemplated the implications of his assumption that citizens of economically dominant countries are free to choose their field of study or career path, while citizens of underdeveloped countries must make choices based on personal pragmatics and national needs (hence, the

great number of engineers). Years later, teaching at the Federal University gave
me deeper insight into Brazil's educational system, which is based on tracked
paths from the point of the entrance examination, mostly moving toward professional degrees, rather than a liberal arts approach that gives students breadth
and allows them to explore and change direction. I have also contemplated the
ways in which the engineer's assumptions were false, imposing a dichotomy
between First and Third World educational options.[16] What he said was not
strictly true; there are many Brazilian anthropologists, some trained abroad and
some trained in Brazil, and though most of them come from relatively privileged
backgrounds, this is not true for all. The engineer also made the assumption
that U.S. students are all middle class or above and have the kinds of economic
liberties that he imagined. In the United States I have often been wistfully told,
"Ah, if I'd studied what I wanted, I would have studied anthropology." The
implication, of course, is that even in the privileged nation of the United States,
students feel constrained by economics and other pragmatics, at least insofar as
they or their parents understand them. (This is even more true today, as more
and more students pursue degrees that are paired to jobs of the same name and
buck at the remaining liberal arts requirements.) To feel free to choose one's
course of study is a different kind of privilege.

The possibility of choosing a field of study based on interest and vocation
rather than evident practicality is conditioned by socioeconomic class and the
related security that one feels in one's future position. Class differences internal
to both the United States and Brazil mean that geographic and social pockets
of First and Third World exist within the other. Not only do some wealthy
Brazilians enjoy all the privileges of the First World and beyond, but some
citizens of the United States do not enjoy any of the advantages that are widely
presumed to exist in that country, whether they be access to health care or
education or a share in the wealth. Those who enjoy the privileges of access in
the United States hold tight to their national myths of equality. The college
students at the university where I teach go on "medical missions" to Honduras
and Ghana to gain valuable experience and personal satisfaction by helping
people in need abroad rather than to nearby inner-city or rural areas or Indian
Health Services, where they would find communities in just as much need but
where they would not be able to preserve their sense of national superiority.
Brazilians, on the other hand, have their own cherished myths, of course, but
they also make a national sport out of mocking their nation's foibles. Like so
many other failures, the extreme inequality that is evident everywhere becomes

"normal," that one-word response Brazilians give to all sorts of outrages: "normal," with a falling intonation, as if to say, "oh well, what did you expect?" They speak freely of "two Brazils," separated by an economic chasm and symbolized in the alliterative contrast between Belgium and Biafra. A Brazilian aphorism states that if you are going to be rich, it is better to be rich in Brazil, but if you are going to be poor, it is better to be poor in the United States—as if it were a matter of choice. I often found my own privileges at odds with the infamous extremes of wealth and poverty in Brazil.

Inequalities

In the 1990s, when I was living in Brazil, the United States was in a period of robust capitalist expansion, an aspiration for "developing" countries, especially for countries like Brazil, in the early phase of transition to a democratic society and about to emerge as one of the BRICS (Brazil, Russia, India, China, and South Africa): countries that held great promise for investors, if not their citizens. Brazil has depths of poverty on a wide scale that are rarely reached in the United States, though years of economic reform had improved the lot of Brazil's poorest, at least until the democratically elected president Dilma Rousseff was ousted in August 2016. The regime headed by Michel Temer reversed the gains of the previous two administrations and plunged forty million people back into abject poverty. The election of Jair Bolsonaro in October 2018 threatens to destabilize the economic and social order in ways unimaginable since the depths of the military dictatorship that he continued to defend throughout the period of democratization.[17] Meanwhile, the United States seems to be moving closer and closer to the kind of economic divide that characterizes the socioeconomic landscape of postcolonial Third World countries. A few moments stand out in my mind as illustrative of the extremes of poverty and their effects.

I could fill pages with stories of encounters with maids. The institution of the "domestic employee" colors Brazilian history, shapes social relations across classes at every level, and is even reflected in architecture (Holston 1989). Maids are ubiquitous, even among lower-middle-class households, to the point that it seems that if you do not hire one then you work as one. My first encounter with a maid was with a twelve-year-old *morena* (African descended with light-brown skin) who worked for my mother-in-law. It was a doubly distressing first encounter with these awkward, intimate relationships. I never fully reconciled myself to these arrangements, simultaneously friendly and strained, supportive and exploitative, familial and yet layered with power inequalities (Goldstein 2003). That my first experience with a Brazilian maid involved a child challenged me to find a role that was sensitive to both cultural and familial dynamics as I came to understand this new social milieu, while I wrestled with the human-rights dilemma of a child laboring to help support her family. She had little formal education and did not understand the use of banks or similar institutions. She would ask me questions, and I would try repeatedly to teach her what she wanted to know, including how to tell time, though in her confusion she would break down in tears. She came to me with questions, such as the time that she wanted to know why Michael Jackson (in the television special about his life broadcast the night before) could speak Portuguese so well if he was also from the United States, or how it was that private moments of his life had been filmed—she did not understand that she had been watching a dubbed dramatization.

No maids lasted long with my mother-in-law. Next came a twenty-three-year-old with long, straight blonde hair and big blue eyes, who was just as poor and had only a second-grade education. I tried again, unsuccessfully, to explain things when she brought me questions, like why a child's disability could not have been caused by the mother seeing a snake during pregnancy. She was older and more confident than the first maid I had met, and also aware of differences of privilege and sensitive about being deceived. Once when I was chopping mushrooms in the kitchen, she asked whether they were the same ones that she had seen growing around town; when I warned her to stay away from those, she assumed that I was suggesting that she was not good enough to eat what I ate, and that I was somehow snubbing her or excluding her from things that were only for people like me. She was right to be sensitive, but it was a dangerous position to take since she could have accidentally poisoned herself to prove a point. The most significant incident came when she decided to ask me about the United States. "You come from the United States, right?" she asked. When I confirmed this, she asked further, "Is the United States as big as São Carlos?" I tried to hide my surprise and explained that the United States was a country, a big country, like Brazil, not a small city (of about one hundred thousand) like São Carlos. The next day she burst into my room with hands on her hips in the indignant posture known as *açucareira* (sugar bowl) and confronted me: "Do you remember what you told me yesterday?" she charged. "That the United States was as big as Brazil?!" Of *course* I remembered. I had tossed and turned into the night thinking about the implications of a grown woman, herself mother to a toddler, not knowing elementary geography, especially when it came to the knowledge of a country that so thoroughly dominated Brazilian politics and broadcast media. I contemplated the meaning of democracy when a significant portion of the population chooses not to vote, as in the United States, and I thought about what that meant for elections in a country where voting is obligatory, as in Brazil. My position had vacillated regarding the advantages and disadvantages of such a policy when poor schools and distorting media meant that the population was not educated enough to make informed decisions at the ballot box. Of *course* I remembered our conversation. "Well," she continued in her high-pitched voice, "I told my husband and he said if it's as big as all that, how come we've never seen pictures of it?!" Then she stormed out again, having put me in my place, leaving me in the wake of her righteous indignation, and probably feeling confident that I would not try to make a fool of her again. The unequal relationship between the United States and Brazil forces Brazilians to know so much more about the United States than the reverse, which means that regardless of whether they are aware of it, Brazilians live under the political and economic shadow of the United States. Her declaration meant that she did not realize that what she saw every night on television in the news and in dubbed movies was from the United States. Of *course* she had seen pictures of the United States, probably every day of her life, but that was not how she understood it. Again, the implications for the system of obligatory voting left me worried, and the moment was a damning indictment of the failed educational system as well, even for those who manage to get some education. Brazil's impoverished citizens bear the brunt of educational policies (and much else) in overcrowded and underfunded schools, undermining the meaning of universal suffrage and the transformative potential of obligatory voting. This everyday social violence has substantive material consequences (Scheper-Hughes 1989), in addition to the explicit violence suffered by poor, mostly Black and Brown communities. I had argued in my youth with fellow political activists about whether voting was exercising a hard-earned right or being complicit in a corrupt system. My thinking about obligatory voting underwent many changes as my experiences in Brazil deepened, especially as I got to know activists who took the long view, foregoing short-term wins for long-term gains, and who credited obligatory voting with the gradual push to the left of the national political agenda. However, a long history of buying votes of the poor and uneducated to the enormous benefit of the very wealthy also hangs over the political process in Brazil. My thoughts on these topics continue to waver, especially as the stranglehold of the oligarchs on the country tightens and as electoral integrity and the status of democracy in the United States are so vulnerable. At the very least, I see clearly how critical education is to any sort of meaningful democracy.

In addition to education, I came to realize that certain basic human needs must be met for people to be able to truly exercise their autonomy as political and social actors. First, I had to come to terms with some unexamined Marxist assumptions.[18] Prior to living in Brazil, I had believed that empirical evidence ("facts") and personal experience provided people with the ability to appraise their circumstances and a capacity and fierce desire to chart their own path to freedom. Though I had never really thought about it consciously, I also apparently believed that there was some lower limit beyond which human dignity would not allow people to sink, and that they would rise up against their oppressors when such a limit was breached.

The first time that I went to Rio de Janeiro all of those assumptions were thrown into turmoil. I accepted the invitation of a student who was taking private English classes with me and who wanted me to accompany her on a visit home. In contrast to the spatial segregation of the poor neighborhoods in the city where I lived, rich and poor in Rio are intertwined, in public space, in private space, and in the very layout of the city, where planned portions of the city displaced the previous residents only to be reoccupied by new poor people building in the newly reconfigured spaces (Carvalho 2013). The self-constructed neighborhoods known as *favelas* fill the fissures and other empty spaces created by urban development schemes in Rio, rather than being on the outskirts as in some other Brazilian cities. A familiar sight in many underdeveloped countries in Latin America and elsewhere, favelas begin when poor people build fragile structures made of found materials in any available space: under overpasses, along roadways, on steep hillsides, and on the edges of some of the wealthiest neighborhoods in Brazil.[19]

I have been asked by Brazilians whether we have favelas in the United States. While we certainly have poor people and poor neighborhoods, the very poor either cannot find housing or cannot afford the rent of public housing or are not well off enough to keep a job or stay in one place. Furthermore, construction regulations make illegal the "auto-construction" that is a defining feature of favelas. Even tent cities or the temporary and visible conglomerations like the "Hoovervilles" of the Great Depression are illegal, though the reasons today usually reference safety codes rather than a recognition of these gatherings as a condemnation of and shameful reflection on politicians in a rich nation. Instead of favelas, we have homeless people, who fall through the cracks rather than filling them.

The dramatic landscape of Rio looks as if the granite monoliths have suddenly jutted up in the midst of an already densely populated area. Instead, the city filled in from the Bay of Guanabara, from the port and the colonial seat of government, displacing first the original inhabitants, and then the emergent neighborhoods of free Black and poor white people. My student's father was a medical doctor and lived in a well-to-do neighborhood built on high ground, safe from the floods brought by torrential tropical rains. A favela was located just up the street, built on the impossibly steep lower slopes of the rock face that rose sharply from there, and the street was busy with the foot traffic of favela residents walking back and forth from the urban center. Increasingly, the upper classes have chosen to forego the autonomy of single-family residences for gated communities and luxury high-rise apartments with armed security, rather than confront the class tensions of such daily proximity (Caldeira 2000). Ironically, this lifestyle nevertheless demands tremendous intimacy across class divides because the upper classes depend entirely on the labor of the poorer classes to cook and clean and garden and care for children and protect them from the rest of the poorer classes. It is a contradictory relationship of mutual interdependence, occasionally tense and hostile but not infrequently intimate and even affectionate.

Toward the end of that first trip to Rio, we drove past Rio's massive landfill, and I was shocked to see that it was teeming with people evidently scouring the mountain of garbage for reusable and recyclable materials. I realized then that abject poverty is not radicalizing or empowering, and that those who must struggle day to day for enough to eat do not have the luxury of planning to overthrow the system. Their dignity is clearly shown in the documentary film *Waste Land* (2010), about the cooperative of *catadores* (trash pickers) who live coincidentally at that same municipal landfill and who worked with Brazilian artist Vik Muniz to create beautiful renditions of famous works of art from trash collected by the *catadores*.[20] Dignity is a state or quality that is quite apart from external conditions.

There is no way to live in such a starkly class-divided social world and not be a participant, not be implicated in it. This is just as true in the United States as it is in Brazil. As a society, we walk past homeless people on the street, forget about Indigenous peoples living in poverty on reservations, avoid certain neighborhoods. We all become numb to the injustices around us, ignoring them so that we can go about our lives. Seeing the injustices is easier when we step outside of the familiar. When I have returned to Brazil for short stays, I break the rules, disrupting the social fabric in ways that I cannot easily afford to do when I am there for longer periods of time (and often relying on the goodwill of friends and other hosts). I sit in the front seat with taxi drivers and ask about economic changes and consumption patterns rather than sitting in the back, absorbed with my phone and isolated. I chat with the security guards in the apartment buildings of well-heeled friends and engage in discussions about the education system. Inevitably, I get the confused question, "Why are you different?" A quick read of my color, my style of dress, and the circumstances of our encounter puts me in one social category, one that my behavior does not fit.[21] In other words, why do I not stay on my side of the class divide? However, I cannot so easily break these social rules during longer stays because continually confronting or resisting the system is an exhausting endeavor. Breaking with these social norms also causes discomfort or even problems for other people. Of course, those in the working classes are not necessarily eager to get cozy with the privileged classes (of which I am presumed to be a part) and are often uncomfortable with my flouting of the norms. That kind of trust takes time to build. On the other hand, those who are privileged do not appreciate having the comfort of their world disturbed and exposed as flimsy, and they are often quick to chide—or worse.

I learned this lesson when visiting the extended family of my fiancé in the northeastern city of Fortaleza, a region known for "traditional" social rules, rooted in the slave economy and *coronelismo*, the corrupt and violent boss system that dominated the agricultural Northeast, the legacy of which is still felt today. Theirs was a landholding family, what might be considered "slumlords" in another context. They still lived in a single-family residence, surrounded by a garden and high wall. I counted nine people in their employ, between full- and part-time: a cook, two maids, a chauffeur, a *passadeira* (a woman whose sole job was to do the ironing), a night guard, a gardener, a manicurist, and a houseboy to whom fell anything that was not covered by the other employees. Between the nine employees, they did not earn even six minimum salaries, nor did they receive any of the common benefits, such as transportation costs, that became required compensation under new labor laws that took effect not long after my visit. The son of the family was being groomed to step into his father's shoes and was already responsible for making the rounds to collect rent. It was to him that the guard appealed for an income increase. My fiancé and I were not supposed to hear the conversation, but it took place right outside the window of the bedroom where we were sleeping. The guard's job was to sit up all night in the garden with a loaded weapon, ready to protect the sleeping family. Rather than make his request face to face, he stood outside the son's window (adjacent to ours) to ask whether he could receive an increase to cover the cost of transportation to and from work. His request was denied. Even more poignant was the situation of the houseboy, a young man from a desperately poor family who lived in what looked like a pile of blankets in a corner of the garage and worked not for a salary but for the cost of his epilepsy medication. Even under these miserable circumstances he was better off than he would have been without the job (as the father of the family explained), if this could really be considered a form of employment as opposed to indentured servitude. Since he picked up the slack around the house, the bulk of the extra work of our stay fell to him, so to thank him we gave him the official jersey of the local Ceará soccer team, of which he was an avid fan. We were roundly chided for this act of reciprocity because, we were told by the family, we had unreasonably raised his expectations. It was a sickening experience. In the face of entrenched systems of unequal power, alliances mean nothing. Friendliness does not put a dent in the system of inequality.

The difference between *having been* to a place and *being* there is in the depth of understanding. In Portuguese, you do not ask a person whether they have been somewhere. You ask whether they "know" the place, no matter how brief the encounter. A tourist can merely pass through a country and then claim to "know" it. Tourists do not have any obligation to acquire foreknowledge. They do not need to study history, socioeconomic hierarchies, the consequences of uneven development, or the legacy of colonial administrations and repressive regimes. Tourists can admire, and buy, and leave with folkloric or artisanal items and postcard memories, without obligations to maintain relations. Theirs is a form of consumption that includes the possibility of just snacking, of savoring tiny bites, and it also gets reproduced at the local level through tourism performances.

One difference between touring and living someplace for an extended period of time—which involves having responsibilities and obligations, time constraints, and financial considerations—is that when one is touring one can afford to give attention to all sorts of things that people who are going about their daily lives cannot. Tourists in Brazil can engage in what Edward Bruner (2005) calls *tourist realism*—that is, they can look at poverty (and even take organized tours to visit favelas),[22] be shocked and offended by it (How can people live this way? How can other people ignore it?), and imagine that they have no connection with or responsibilities toward the obvious inequalities (Freire-Medeiros 2013). This would seem to be the inverse of the *imperialist nostalgia* described by Renato Rosaldo (1989): rather than lamenting and longing for a past that one has had a hand in destroying, one may feel a sense of superiority and a self-satisfied clear conscience that comes with imagining that one is not implicated in another's suffering. However, the only way that this imagining is possible is by deliberately ignoring—being ignorant of—the larger patterns of inequality that are reproduced at the global, national, and regional levels.

Homecomings

When the opportunity arose to teach anthropology at the Federal University, I knew that I had to fix my legal status (in order to be a federal government employee!), and my fiancé and I finally married, four years after I had arrived in Brazil; the man handling our documents was clearly galled that he could only fine me the maximum penalty for overstaying my visa, a small punishment for such a gross violation, and far less expensive than if I had done what I was supposed to do and regularly returned to the United States or traveled anywhere out of the country to renew my visa.

Significantly, it was teaching anthropology that pulled me back to myself, reminded me of who I was, and eventually helped me extract myself from that troubled relationship. One day it hit me that I had been gone for half a decade without so much as a visit home, and I knew that I had to leave. I had to borrow money from a friend for the ticket.

Less than a year later I was back, this time on my own terms, to conduct dissertation research. My scholarly work focuses on meaning and belonging for transnational peoples—Garifunas on the Caribbean coast of Guatemala and Jews from many countries of origin in Brazil—looking at the relationship between ethnic identity and national identity.[23] Transnational identities make sense to me because my family is spread out across the North American continent and multiple nations (both siblings and cousins have other citizenships) and because my personal experiences have led me to reside in multiple countries. Beyond the U.S. citizenship that I acquired by virtue of my place of birth, I have gained and lost legal resident status in three other countries so far in my life.

For years I was a landed immigrant in Canada, where my father lives, until the Canadian government finally made me choose to either live in Canada or give it up. I also briefly had temporary immigrant status in England that allowed me to work. In Brazil, I could have eventually parlayed my status into dual citizenship had I been more strategic about it, but after completing fieldwork I did not return often enough to maintain the hard-earned equivalent of a green card that I had acquired after paying my fines (though I did not stay long enough to actually receive the official card). My travels to Brazil now require a visa, as if I had never lived there.[24]

Travelers expect culture shock when they go abroad. They expect the unfamiliar, the strange, the disorienting.[25] They expect to not understand. They also enjoy the "security of a known return" (Harrison 2003, 140), something that I did not have for most of the time I lived in Brazil. What is less well known is the experience of culture shock upon returning home after a long absence. While finding that home has changed is disconcerting, even more disorienting is discovering that what was familiar and comfortable is no longer so.

When I left the United States in 1992, Bill Clinton had just been elected but had not yet taken office. I missed most of his administration and returned in time to catch the Monica Lewinsky scandal. When I left there was no internet, no cell phones, and no SUVs, and I returned to a coastal California utterly transformed by the economic bubble. In Southern California, the real estate market was moving so fast that people were buying houses in a matter of hours and offering $100,000 over the asking price. I was so repulsed by the conspicuous consumption that I took the gold Mercedes-Benz as the ultimate symbol of disregard for the rest of the world, and they were everywhere, so I counted them, to the irritation of those around me. Heading back to my graduate program in Berkeley, I found that the price for rentals had tripled; the graduate advisor joked that I could find a piano box to sleep in. I was flat broke, having left Brazil with no money, only the personal belongings that I could carry in two suitcases. I had not accompanied the rising costs, and I was panicked.

I was not only economically but culturally out of step. I did not get jokes (my mother had to explain popular culture to me), I could not remember how to pump gas (self-service eliminates jobs, so in Brazil employees pump gas, make photocopies, and so forth), and I was completely overwhelmed by the conspicuous abundance and the excess of (false) choices that are offered up everywhere, especially in grocery stores.[26] When people were confused that I did not know about something, I explained that I had "been away" (I thought that it sounded snobby to say that I had been "abroad" or out of the country), until a friend told me that "away" made it sound as if I had been institutionalized. Additionally, and perhaps most strangely, I no longer spoke English like a native speaker. I had spent so much time exclusively in Portuguese that I am certain my brain's pathways had changed. I ended up speaking a rather "creative" form of English, continually finding myself in grammatical cul-de-sacs, and translating Portuguese expressions into English on the fly. My family and friends teased me when I came up with odd word choices—understandable but not standard English. The only person who really understood what I was doing was a perfectly bilingual Brazilian friend who knew which Portuguese words and expressions I was employing.

It has been two decades since that first shock of return, and I still feel it on a daily basis. I have filled in most of the gaps in my knowledge of popular culture and have gotten more adept at recognizing and smoothing over any that still exist. However, the transformation that I experienced is not reversible. Ultimately, the transformation that I felt was not only about language or cultural knowledge: it was about perspective.

I was in Brazil for a short trip in 2003 when the United States invaded Iraq. I watched the coverage of the bombing of Baghdad on CNN International in the hotel and the airport. My flight arrived in Miami at four in the morning when the only sign of life at the airport was on the televisions showing CNN's continuous war coverage. Even though I was watching coverage of the same war, it seemed as if instead of an airplane I had entered a history-changing machine like the time-machine elevator invented by Ray Bradbury. Although I had been following the news, the coverage was completely different, as if it were a different war. Certainly, from the point of view of the United States, it was a different war than it was for the rest of the world.

While living in Rio as faculty-in-residence for my university's study center there, during the 2016 elections, I was intensely aware of the global anxiety about our elections in the United States. Most people in the United States pay little attention to any but the most publicized elections in other countries. However, upon hearing me speak in English with my family, total strangers would ask whether I was voting for Trump, and then whether I thought there was a chance he would win. Over and over, people told me that because U.S. policy has such impact on the rest of the world, everyone in the world should be allowed to vote in U.S. elections. They cannot afford to ignore what goes on in the country that dominates global politics.

I have had the privilege of travel, of extended stays in other countries, and of immersion in social worlds other than the ones in which I was raised. Though often difficult, these experiences are transformative and enriching. According to a fundamental principle of relativity, one's place in social or physical space influences how one apprehends the world. This place is not a momentary or literal thing but rather an enduring part of the accumulated experiences that make us who we are. If our experiences shape who we are, they also locate us in the social world and inform our perspective. My experiences in Brazil fundamentally transformed me; from my perspective, the very shape of the world changed.

Notes

1. Thanks to a 1907 arrangement between the Japanese and Brazilian governments, Brazil is home to the largest population of Japanese descendants outside of Japan. They mostly reside in the city of São Paulo. See Lesser 2003.
2. Brazil's indebtedness to Britain began in 1808, when the Portuguese royal family fled Napoleon's advancing army and set up the royal court in Rio de Janeiro; during their passage across the Atlantic, with the entire court and royal records, they were protected by the British.
3. Italians were first large wave of immigrants following the end of slavery in 1888 (Brazil was the last nation in the Americas to prohibit slavery). As I said above, the town was far from homogeneous, being home to people of both Japanese and African descent as well as a handful of European expats. Candomblé *terreiros* (centers of worship for this Afro-Brazilian religion) existed alongside Kardecist/ spiritist centers and other syncretic Brazilian religious entities. However, Roman Catholicism was hegemonic, even materially so, with the cathedral at the center of town.
4. Brazil invested in ethanol long before most had heard of it in the United States. It was a way for the country to gain some economic independence before the discovery of massive oil reserves off the coast of Rio de Janeiro.
5. Oklahoman spoken-word poet Lauren Zuniga's line from her "Poem to Progressives Plotting Mass Exodus" echoes in my head: "You resent even the dirt for being so damn red."
6. Brazil was still in the early days of the transition to democracy after military rule. I discuss this transition in the next section. For helpful introductions to Brazil's political and social history, see Skidmore 2009 and Eakin 2017. For an analysis of Brazil since the dictatorship, see McCann 2008.
7. Ford is one of several foreign automobile companies that produce vehicles in Brazil for the Brazilian market and was one of the early U.S. companies to put down roots in Brazil, even before Roosevelt's Good Neighbor Policy. In one of the stranger chapters in U.S.-Brazilian relations, Henry Ford established a massive community

("colony" would be more accurate) in the Amazon to extract rubber. He called this community "Fordlandia" (Grandin 2010).

8. These stories include misunderstandings between Portuguese and Spanish but also between Brazilian Portuguese and Continental Portuguese, and they overlap with a joke cycle about Portuguese people, a favorite target of Brazilian humor.

9. This sort of sudden temperature drop impresses me less now that I live in Oklahoma with even wilder weather.

10. While *jeitinho* can refer to skirting rules and getting around bureaucracies, finding a way around things can also mean making creative repairs, a necessary skill when parts are unavailable or expensive, also called *gambiarra*. In this sense, it is similar to the English-language verb *MacGyver*, based on the title character of the television series of the same name, meaning to make an improvised and inventive repair with materials at hand.

11. High inflation marked the period immediately following the military dictatorship (some scholars have argued that it was one of the motivations for the military to step aside), and President Collor's decision to freeze bank accounts to try to control inflation was one of the reasons for his loss of popularity. During high inflation, salaries and bank accounts would get "adjustments" at the end of every month, but the gain was lost by the time that workers received their pay. Prices in stores were adjusted daily, so comparison shopping was pointless, and cash lost value, so people used checks as much as possible. Credit cards were not yet widely used.

12. Counting on his previous popularity, Collor had called on the population to give him a show of support by turning out in the streets wearing the national colors of green and yellow; Brazilians filled the streets wearing black instead. This action was all the more remarkable because it predated social media and the phenomenon of flash mobs. I had imagined that I would see more of this collective exuberance.

13. Latin American soap operas, or *novelas*, are cultural staples—especially the Brazilian and Mexican ones with their high production value and potent cultural themes. See Benavides 2008 on the high drama of Mexican *novelas*.

14. *Explode Coração* roughly translates as Bursting Heart. It is an expression that refers to being ready to burst with anticipation, and it is also the title of a song by the Brazilian artist Gonzaguinha and also recorded by other artists. The *novela* ran on the Globo television network in 1995–96.

15. Erica Williams's (2013) analysis of the ways in which Brazil, and especially the city of Salvador, Bahia, is racialized as Black in transnational discourse is a useful counterpoint; like Babb (2011), Williams interrogates the characterization of tourism as necessarily exploitative. She instead suggests ways in which the toured can exert their own agency to take advantage of the personally transformative potential of tourism, despite the intersections of race, class, gender, and nation. Parallels can also be drawn to Jennifer Roth-Gordon's (2017) explication of the racialization of space, whether the Blackness of the *morros* (hills, favelas) or the whiteness of the *asfalto* (asphalt, the streets of the South Zone).

16. The terms *First World* and *Third World* are vestiges of the Cold War. *First World* refers to the "developed" capitalist countries of what today is known as the Global North. *Third World* refers to "developing" countries, generally in the Global South. The relationship of these terms to the Cold War is clearer when we consider their less-widely known counterpart, the *Second World*, which refers to the socialist-communist industrialized nations of China and the Soviet bloc. The *Fourth World* was added later to refer to Indigenous peoples, nations within these nations. All these terms are politically problematic, suggestive of the evolutionary logic that often underlies such schema (i.e., the notion of progress implied in the idea of development), and inadequate for describing complex, historically contingent, global interrelations. Though less widely known outside the academy, approaches that emphasize historical flows of power and capital—such as world systems theory (Wallerstein 1974, 2004)—are generally more accurate. Related approaches include dependency theory (Cardoso 1972) and the theory of underdevelopment (Frank [1966] 1970), with their concepts of center and periphery, or metropolis and satellite, to describe nested relations of power and extraction. These theories also lend themselves more easily to revisions that recognize flows in multiple directions, including between nations of the periphery (i.e., South–South). For more on different sorts of global "flows," see Appadurai 1996.

17. In March 2019, President Jair Bolsonaro ordered the Defense Ministry to commemorate the fifty-fifth anniversary of coup on March 31, 1964.

18. Geographer Michael Johns (2012) discusses how his experiences in Nicaragua during the Sandinista Revolution transformed the assumptions that he had held, assumptions based more on theory than on practice.

19. In other Latin American countries, these (initially) informal neighborhoods are known by other terms: *comunidades nuevas, colonias, pueblos jóvenes, villas miserias,* and *campamentos*, among others. These terms vary in the degree to which they carry pejorative meaning and reflect local histories and conditioning factors.

20. In a related vein, the documentary *Landfill Harmonic* (2015) features an orchestra of poor children in Paraguay who play classical music on instruments fashioned from materials pulled from a dump.

21. Roth-Gordon (2017) describes this process of reading racialized bodies, a complicated calculus of physiognomic and social factors.

22. This global phenomenon of *pro-poor tourism* or *pity tourism* (but popularly known as *poorism*) is a form of *reality tour* (Freire-Medeiros 2009), which itself is a special kind of *cultural tourism*. Rather than seeking "'the picturesque' or 'local color'" in the traditional or folkloric (Smith 1989, 4–5), international tourists seek "authenticity" in organized visits to poor areas or neighborhoods. In cultural tourism, poor people "become objects of study *per se*" (Smith 1989, 5). Freire-Medeiros (2009) cautions that favela tours, some of which may be framed as *social tours* through their emphasis on helping, may rather be closer to *dark tours*, which commodify and spectacularize destruction and violence. Certainly, the municipal government in Rio did not embrace the representation of Brazil through the favela

when Michael Jackson and Spike Lee showed up in 1996 to film Jackson's music video "They Don't Care About Us" (Freire-Medeiros 2013). However, by the time that Brazil was positioning itself, and Rio in particular, for the mega-events of the early twenty-first century (Pan American Games, World Cup, and the Olympics), the favela (as image and commodity) was in full force as representative of the "real" Brazil. Further, in favela tourism, the contrast between the heightened mobility of the tourist and the lack of social mobility of the favela resident has been intensified by the recent construction of aerial cable cars in several favelas in Rio, ostensibly created to ease access and mobility of residents but functioning as a means for tourists to behold Rio's breathtaking views (Freire-Medeiros 2015). Popular films such as *City of God* (2002) transform the favela into a commodity to be consumed rather than a place to visit—but they do this through spectacularizing violence (Robb Larkins 2015, 110). Tourists are not educated through these visits to the favelas, as a 2015 encounter with an Australian tourist in an Ipanema hotel reminded me. Wearing a T-shirt decorated in a style known as "favela chic" (which aestheticizes poverty through representations of the characteristic blocks of houses on clothes and other fashion items), this tourist had gone on a favela tour the day before. When I asked him which favela (out of hundreds in Rio) he had visited, he looked at me blankly and then blurted out, "The safe one!"

23. I published this ethnographic work as a book. See Klein 2012.

24. When I lived in Brazil for the 2016–17 academic year, I discovered that I am still in the system and that my Brazilian identification number (CPF) remains.

25. Culture shock or disorientation can also occur within a country. I live in Oklahoma now, and even after more than a decade, longer than I have lived anywhere in my life, I am still a "resident alien," a term a colleague used to refer to the difficult relationship many transplanted faculty at the university have with our adopted home.

26. By "(false) choices" I mean the plethora of options that we have as citizen-consumers in the United States, most of which are not meaningful options. I consider these choices, alongside the displays of abundance, to be ideological—that is, to be expressions of ideas that we have about "freedom," among other expressed values. For example, the toothpaste aisle in any supermarket will have an array of formulas, each promising a slightly different sort of cleaning, available in several flavors and sizes. These same choices are also offered by other brands, and the entire thing takes up the better part of the aisle, presenting the illusion of abundance and choice: freedom. None of these options make much of a difference in the function of the toothpaste, and we do not have choices that are significantly different.

References

Appadurai, Arjun. 1996. *Modernity at Large: Cultural Dimensions of Globalization*. Minneapolis: University of Minnesota Press.

Babb, Florence E. 2011. *The Tourism Encounter: Fashioning Latin American Nations and Histories*. Stanford, Calif.: Stanford University Press.

Babb, Florence E. 2012. "Theorizing Gender, Race, and Cultural Tourism in Latin America." *Latin American Perspectives* 39 (6): 36–50.

Barbosa, Lívia Neves de H. 1995. "The Brazilian Jeitinho: An Exercise in National Identity." In *The Brazilian Puzzle: Culture on the Borderlands of the Western World*, edited by David J. Hess and Roberto DaMatta, 35–48. New York: Columbia University Press.

Benavides, O. Hugo. 2008. *Drugs, Thugs and Divas: Telenovelas and Narco-Dramas in Latin America*. Austin: University of Texas Press.

Bruner, Edward M. 2005. *Culture on Tour: Ethnographies of Travel*. Chicago: University of Chicago Press.

Caldeira, Teresa P. R. 2000. *City of Walls: Crime, Segregation, and Citizenship in São Paulo*. Berkeley: University of California Press.

Cardoso, Fernando Henrique. 1972. "Dependency and Development in Latin America." *New Left Review* 74: 83–95.

Carvalho, Bruno. 2013. *Porous City: A Cultural History of Rio de Janeiro*. Liverpool: Liverpool University Press.

DaMatta, Roberto. 1993. "Antropologia da Saudade." In *Conta de Mentiroso: Sete Ensaios de Antropologia Brasileira*. Rio de Janeiro: Rocco.

Eakin, Marshall C. 2017. *Becoming Brazilians: Race and National Identity in Twentieth-Century Brazil*. Cambridge: Cambridge University Press.

Frank, Andre Gunder. (1966) 1970. "The Development of Underdevelopment." In *Imperialism and Underdevelopment*, edited by Robert I. Rhodes, 4–17. New York: Monthly Review Press.

Freire-Medeiros, Bianca. 2009. "The Favela and Its Touristic Transits." *Geoforum* 40: 580–88.

Freire-Medeiros, Bianca. 2013. *Touring Poverty*. New York: Routledge.

Freire-Medeiros, Bianca. 2015. "'Peace, Love, and Fun': An Aerial Cable Car and the Traveling Favela." In *Transport, Mobility, and the Production of Urban Space*, edited by Julie Cidell and David Prytherch, 263–77. New York: Routledge.

Goldstein, Donna. 2003. *Laughter out of Place: Race, Class, Violence, and Sexuality in a Rio Shantytown*. Berkeley: University of California Press.

Grandin, Greg. 2010. *Fordlandia: The Rise and Fall of Henry Ford's Forgotten Jungle City*. New York: Picador.

Harris, Marvin D. 1964. "Racial Identity in Brazil." *Luso-Brazilian Review* 1 (2): 21–28.

Harrison, Julia. 2003. *Being a Tourist: Finding Meaning in Pleasure Travel*. Vancouver: University of British Columbia Press.

Holston, James. 1989. *The Modernist City: An Anthropological Critique of Brasília*. Chicago: University of Chicago Press.

Johns, Michael. 2012. *The Education of a Radical: An American Revolutionary in Sandinista Nicaragua*. Austin: University of Texas Press.

Klein, Misha. 2012. *Kosher Feijoada and Other Paradoxes of Jewish Life in São Paulo*. Gainesville: University Press of Florida.

Lesser, Jeffrey, ed. 2003. *Searching for Home Abroad: Japanese Brazilians and Transnationalism*. Durham, N.C.: Duke University Press.

McCann, Bryan. 2008. *The Throes of Democracy: Brazil Since 1989*. Halifax, N.S.: Fernwood.

O'Dougherty, Maureen. 2002. *Consumption Intensified: The Politics of Middle-Class Daily Life in Brazil*. Durham, N.C.: Duke University Press.

Robb Larkins, Erika. 2015. *The Spectacular Favela: Violence in Modern Brazil*. Berkeley: University of California Press.

Rosaldo, Renato. 1989. "Imperialist Nostalgia." *Representations* 26: 107–22.

Roth-Gordon, Jennifer. 2017. *Race and the Brazilian Body: Blackness, Whiteness, and Everyday Language in Rio de Janeiro*. Oakland: University of California Press.

Scheper-Hughes, Nancy. 1989. *Death Without Weeping: The Violence of Everyday Life in Brazil*. Berkeley: University of California Press.

Skidmore, Thomas. 2009. *Brazil: Five Centuries of Change*. 2nd ed. Oxford: Oxford University Press.

Smith, Valene L. 1989. Introduction to *Hosts and Guests: The Anthropology of Tourism*, 2nd ed., edited by Valene Smith, 1–17. Philadelphia: University of Pennsylvania Press.

Wallerstein, I. 1974. "The Rise and Future Demise of the World Capitalist System: Concepts for Comparative Analysis." *Comparative Studies in Society and History* 16 (4): 387–415.

Wallerstein, I. 2004. *World-Systems Analysis: An Introduction*. Durham, N.C.: Duke University Press.

Williams, Erica Lorraine. 2013. *Sex Tourism in Bahia: Ambiguous Entanglements*. Urbana: University of Illinois Press.

TWO

The Ethnographic Traveler

Immersions, Encounters, and Imaginings

JUAN ANTONIO FLORES MARTOS

> *I thought that woman was crazy. But by now I wasn't think-*
> *ing at all. I felt as in a faraway world and I let myself go. My*
> *body, which seemed to loosen up, was being completely surren-*
> *dered, it had let go its reins and anyone could play with it as*
> *if it were a rag.*
>
> —JUAN RULFO, *PEDRO PÁRAMO*

In *Pedro Páramo* (Rulfo [1955] 1994), the main character, Juan Preciado, grapples with a feeling of otherworldliness as he searches for his dead father in the
village of Comalá, a metaphor for the world of the dead. Ethnographic fieldwork can take us on a similar journey, where we struggle to distinguish dreams
from reality. Yet we rarely discuss how this profound disorientation hampers
trust, resurrects past encounters and misunderstandings, and shapes our dreams.
Rather than making rational sense of such extraordinary phenomena, I pro-
pose that we are better off surrendering to them, trusting that our feelings and
visions will lead us in a direction that ultimately reveals much about ourselves
and the worlds we live in. As ethnographers, we are often assumed to be a particular type of traveler who develops social and personal relationships for the
sake of research. The assumption that ethnographers are in full control of their
interactions and tasks during fieldwork, however, is false. Truth be told, our
work is highly conditioned by chance, circumstance, and emotion. This chapter
calls attention to the emotions—rather than "information"—that result from
uncomfortable, awkward, even conflictual moments between anthropologists,
locals, and travelers (Davies and Spencer 2010).[1] Through my reflections on
fieldwork in Mexico in the 1990s and recent encounters in Bolivia, I highlight

moments where curiosity leads to pleasure, interrogations signal distrust, guilt can lead to catharsis, and dreams reflect deep-seated fears.

Curiosity/Pleasure

Like tourism, which relies on the performance of the exotic (Salazar 2010), ethnographic encounters involve imagination and fantasy. While travel evokes a sense of curiosity, feelings of discovery, and the pleasure of new experiences, these sentiments are typically attributed to those who do the traveling. What kinds of pleasures do people who host travelers experience? Through a focus on fieldwork in Veracruz, I consider the attitude and actions undertaken by "hosts" as they organize their lives partly around travelers. How are visitors treated and perceived by various hosts? What do locals find curious about travelers, and what kinds of responses do they inspire? In fully characterizing the guest/host interaction, I aim to recognize the critical role that local people play in shaping travel and research experiences.

With each visit (I have traveled to Veracruz seven times since 1993), the strange became familiar. During the years in which I conducted fieldwork (from 1993 through 1997), Veracruz reflected on a smaller scale the intense crises facing Mexico: a political crisis as the dominance of the Institutional Revolutionary Party (PRI) waned, an economic crisis as the extreme devaluation of the peso and massive job losses occurred, and a social crisis as insecurity and violence rose, disproportionately affecting the working class and middle class. When I returned in 1996 and 1997, I noticed that my relationships with the residents of the port city of Veracruz, referred to locally as *porteños*, were transformed by a process that I call *de-exoticization*. At first *porteños* assumed, because I was a Spaniard, that both national and class differences existed between us. Although my nationality helped facilitate a number of interviews as well as access to exclusive places in the city, it also marked me as foreign. Locals assume that most Spaniards are retailers, businessmen always looking to make a profit. Given the power of this stereotype, I had to reassure them that I was not trying to profit from our relationship. I encountered this stereotype during festive occasions when *porteños'* alcohol consumption led to violent threats against me. I reminded them that I was "a different kind of Spaniard" than those they met in Veracruz. Eventually, as my relationships with locals deepened, I could no longer pretend to be an "ignorant and incompetent foreigner."

As a foreigner, I was also lumped in with stereotypes of North Americans. In the common slang of Veracruz, North Americans and Western foreigners are called *gabachos*. Locals use the expression "going to the Gabacho," for crossing the U.S.-Mexican border. To call someone a *gabachero* or *gabachera* means that he or she likes to interact with foreign people in a friendly or even sexual manner. The prostitutes who offer their services to foreigners are also called *gabacheras/os*, as are those, like tourist guides, musicians, clerks, bohemians, or carefree individuals, who invest a great amount of time in meeting, hanging out with, or sexually interacting with foreigners. To men in Veracruz, a *gabachera* also represents a desirable feminine body that is surrendered to or possessed by a foreigner. George, a friend who lived in the port of Veracruz, explained. He portrayed Ronnie—a *porteño* thought to be a *gabachero*—in the following manner:

> Here foreigners are called *gabachos*, and Ronnie, who has always been a ladies' man, is a *gabachero* because he likes to hang around foreign women, *gringas*, and conquer their hearts. He's always around the parish checking things out, and when he sees a foreign woman he likes, she never gets away. He doesn't stop until he gets her.

Likewise, travelers may seek intimacy as a type of eroticized and intensified sociability (Harrison 2003). My sexuality and intimate desires were central to my experience as a tourist and ethnographer. As a European, I was similarly positioned by Veracruz women across the age spectrum. Since European men were painted as "very liberal," local women sought relationships with them. While joking or flirting with me, Veracruz women alluded to this sexuality. According to Susan Frohlick (2013), intimacy is a fluid transnational terrain where social control and desire are negotiated. In the global sexual cartography of Veracruz's port, my status as a European tourist became problematic when my social conduct did not conform to this stereotype, even leading to a rumor that I was gay.

In addition to pursuing foreigners, *gabacheras/os* often hook up with tourists who are actively seeking sex, creating what anthropologist Octávio Sacramento (2017) has called *transatlantic intimacy projects*. Based on social and sexual interaction between European tourists and Brazilian women on a beach (Ponta Negra) in the Brazilian state of Natal, Sacramento describes the bodies, desires, and emotions that create a "global beach" milieu and underpin sexual tourism. Sacramento interrogates how romantic and/or physical engagement might transgress numerous boundaries (territorial, political, ethnic, sexual, civic, racial, and class). Where journalists and outsiders tend to speak only of sexual exploitation, economic interests, and humiliation, particularly in considering local women, Sacramento finds that some women are motivated to establish relationships with travelers because they are treated well. Similar practices have long formed part of the cultural landscape of the port of Veracruz. A *porteña* named Betty was engaged in such transatlantic projects. Her boyfriends and acquaintances over the years included an Israelite, an Italian, a Spaniard, and a Canadian. With some, she maintained direct, in-person relationships. With others, she had more intermittent affairs through the mail or by telephone. At one point she moved from Veracruz to Houston, Texas, where she got a job as a preschool and art teacher. During this time, she maintained contact with several international lovers. Another woman, Amanda, had relationships with local men as well as other Mexicans (on vacation in Veracruz), Italians, Canadians, and Spaniards. She ended up marrying a U.S. citizen and moving with him to New Hampshire for a time, and she now lives in a small town in Florida. For Amanda and many others in Veracruz, emotional, corporeal, even sexual association with foreigners is a long-standing practice.

These global intimate encounters traffic in transcultural emotions, fantasies, affections, and desires, and they must be acknowledged as part of our ethnographic experience. While I have not been tempted to take part in such a transatlantic project, I know researchers who have been intimate with local residents while conducting fieldwork. Some of these encounters have even led to successful relocations, marriages, and families, something not always dealt with—at least in more of an emotional sense—in the scholarly literature. By thinking through the relations between hosts and guests, I call attention to a corporeal geography of travel.

Interrogations/Distrust

Nelson Graburn (1977) argued that tourism was a kind of ritual or a form of modern pilgrimage. Similarly, ethnographers consider fieldwork to be a rite of passage. My first fieldwork forays did not go smoothly; they involved interrogations as a form of hazing, another kind of ritual. On my first visit to the southern state of Oaxaca, Mexico, in 1989 to collect material for my doctoral thesis, I made contact with colleagues at the National Indigenous Institute's (INI) regional centers (Centros Coordinadores Indigenistas or CCIs). I hoped to gain an introduction to the Indigenous communities of San Mateo del Mar and San Juan Guichicovi, both located in the tropical Tehuantepec Isthmus. I expected to cultivate relationships with community members who would become collaborators in my future research. As it turned out, community members ended up asking me all types of questions. To my chagrin, I became the interviewee as I experienced the asymmetry in power relations propagated by field research.

During my stay in San Juan Guichicovi, a Mixe community located in the low sierra, next to Juchitán, I met Virgilio Jiménez, who was a Mixe bilingual teacher of Indigenous popular culture at the Dirección General de Culturas Populares (DGCP)[2] and—as I later learned—a member of the Unión de Comunidades Indígenas de la Zona Norte del Istmo (UCIZONI), an organization associated with the long-standing Zapatista rebellion in the region. Jiménez kindly invited me to visit UCIZONI's headquarters. Although I had not yet decided exactly what to ask, I wanted to know more about the context, problems, and priorities of the organization in order to contrast his and other members' perspectives with "official" data provided to me by the INI national headquarters. Following the advice of a Mexican anthropologist, I brought Corona beers to the meeting. When I arrived, Jiménez introduced me to seven of his UCIZONI colleagues, nearly all of whom were DGCP teachers. As we prepared to talk, they assumed a serious, "strictly business" expression as they sat across from me. One man began asking questions, starting what I soon realized would become a full-blown interrogation. I introduced myself as a graduate student interested in exploring the region, but my explanation was not convincing. The UCIZONI crew persisted in knowing why I was in San Juan. What I was looking for? Who were my contacts in town? What had I been told about the area? Was I really a student? How many days did I plan to stay, and what exactly I was going to be doing? Understandably, they were suspicious. They shared that they had negative experiences with anthropologists from Mexico City and from abroad. They told me, for example, of a Swiss anthropologist who had done research on traditional herbs and Mixe medicine but had not given anything back to the community. They asked me whether I would do the same after completing my research.

I could tell from their line of questioning that they also suspected me of being some kind of undercover agent. Maybe I worked for the CIA or perhaps the Mexican government? At the time, members of UCIZONI had been threatened and attacked; they blamed the federal government. Although their queries were cast in a somewhat friendly manner, the situation was tense. Alone in their company, I began to fear that they could dispose of me at any moment. Jiménez told me days later that the group picked up on my initial feelings of hesitation and fear. For this reason, they suspected that I might be a police or government informant. They were also thrown off by my Canadian baseball hat.

Ultimately, however, I passed this initial test, after which we opened the beers that I had brought and drank to our new acquaintanceship, a sign that I had gained the trust of the group. Once I was fully welcomed, our conversation took on a decidedly different tone as we began to discuss matters of a more confidential and sensitive nature. I learned that local caciques had killed several members of their community and that many community members feared for their lives. Jiménez and the others told me how political struggles had allowed outside enemies to infiltrate and negatively influence the life of the community.

That same year I also worked for a week with a Spanish archaeological team excavating at the archaeological site of Oxkintoc in the Yucatán Peninsula, near the town of Maxcanú. After I had spent several days at the dig, my longing for adventure took over. I was told that some two hours from Maxcanú was Hacienda Paraíso, a major center of henequen production before the Mexican Revolution. One of the camp's archaeologists had been there and had become fascinated with the hacienda's chapel façade, to which he had cleverly attached excavated Mayan sculptures, engravings, and other valuable objects that he had found in nearby ruins in order for them not to be plundered.

My colleague told me that the only way to get there—as bizarre as it seems—was to talk to the owner of a brothel in Maxcanú and rent an old bicycle that a client had left behind. I followed his instructions, secured the bike, and—after almost two hours cycling down a dirt road in the pouring rain—reached Hacienda Paraíso. The place was a small community made up of traditional Mayan houses with thatched roofs surrounded by what remained of the old hacienda's foundation, now all blackened and covered in vegetation. On arrival I asked for the sacristan (sexton) and was told that he was out working with the bees but would be back soon. I then made my way to a large terrace covered with a thatched roof. Seeing me, some young men immediately came over and started asking all types of questions. I must have appeared quite alien to them: a tired and sweaty gringo, totally wet from the rain and riding up to their small village on an old bicycle. Without initially realizing it, I was again subject to an informal interrogation. First, these young men wanted to know whether I was some kind of preacher whose aim was to convert them to a new faith. (Later I learned that the village played host not only to traditional Catholics but to a number of Jehovah's Witnesses and Presbyterians). They also wanted to know whether I worked for the government or was an informant, detective, or spy of some sort. When I told them who I was, they seemed to find it difficult to believe that I had not come to proselytize or conduct a criminal investigation. Similarly, they had a hard time believing me when I told them I had absolutely no interest in stealing pre-Hispanic objects attached to the walls of the church or other valuables to be found in the Santa Barbara ruins three kilometers away. Why in the world would anyone come to Hacienda Paraíso if not for these very reasons?

The most active interrogator was Guadalupe Chan, a twenty-year-old father of three whose grandfather was the local ritual specialist. Upon shedding his initial suspicion of me, he spoke to me more than the others did. During the two days that I stayed there, he and I developed a close relationship. Chan told me about events that had taken place in the village. He spoke of numerous attempted robberies of the pre-Hispanic sculptures. Chan also shared how his grandfather had once been frightened when hearing the sound of drums coming from the archaeological ruins. In this and other encounters, my enduring intense questioning was an indispensable aspect of my gaining trust and subsequently establishing a relationship with local people. Without this test, I simply would not have been privy to information and stories such as those narrated by Chan.

I traveled to Bolivia in 2002. At the time, Bolivia was facing a social crisis, reflected by a political scene dominated by a "contractual democracy" and a strong reliance on international and American NGOs. The country elected as president Gonzalo Sánchez de Lozada, a member of the Revolutionary Nationalist Movement (MNR) party, with the Movement for Socialism (MAS) party, to which Evo Morales belonged, coming in second place. The media engaged in daily coverage of popular struggles and social movements. I was there to participate in an intercultural project studying the relationship between biomedical practitioners and traditional Kallawaya healers near the town of Charazani in the northwestern part of Bolivia. This endeavor would lead to one of the most unexpected and intense interrogations I have ever experienced while conducting fieldwork. Entering the medical post of San Pedro Curva, I met up with Pedro Mamani, a twenty-eight-year-old Bolivian physician. Despite his relatively young age, Mamani was an experienced doctor, who worked with a team of similarly experienced practitioners (a dentist and two nursing assistants) in the heart of the Kallawaya region. I asked whether I could interview them. Pedro accepted, but in front of the other nurses, and before I could turn on my recorder, he started asking me questions about my status as a foreign researcher and my purpose for being there. Who was I? What exactly was I hoping to find? Who was I working for? Who had financed my project? How much money was I being paid? Where were my observations going to be published? And perhaps most critically: What was I going to give back to the community as compensation for their time, information, and confidence?

Somewhat taken aback, I tried to answer with as much honesty and detail as I could. Initially, our interaction was tense, his manner stern, but little by little, our conversation loosened up. Only after a period of exhausting and intense interrogation did Mamani accept to be formally interviewed. What ultimately ensued was a fascinating discussion on health issues: the lack of resources, institutional abandonment, collaboration with traditional Kallawaya healers, and the ethical and political dilemmas of working as a doctor in Indigenous communities. As anthropologists we rarely receive training on how to manage or proceed in these situations. So it is easy to exclude from our publications encounters that are filled with tension or that manifest disinterest,[3] conversations that failed to take place or produce a substantive outcome. This erasure points to the fragility of personal and communicative relationships during fieldwork.

My age and inexperience was the cause of much of the initial tension in our meeting, but experiencing this tension and "interrogation" helped me better understand the doctor's viewpoint and the oppressive conditions of the region. As Pierre Bourdieu (1999) points out in *The Weight of the World*, interviews reflect asymmetric relations (social, symbolic, and power) and constitute a violent form of communication. As a result of this encounter and similar interrogations that I faced during my fieldwork, I have taken greater care since to avoid reinforcing asymmetric relations and propagating symbolic violence, and I have worked to cultivate an ethical and methodological awareness of my role as ethnographer. In addition, being "interrogated" as a visiting anthropologist has taught me several things. Questions coming from a stranger can cause fear and suspicion. Local people have their own questions, which the researcher must address in order to earn their trust. They have the right to research us. Being interrogated proved a key element in a process of mutual recognition and respect, and it became a requisite for communication across cultures. In a sense, these interrogations constituted moments of alternative contact, spaces of critical exchange that called attention to ethical quandaries and asymmetric relations of power between myself and community members (Lai and Smith 2010). Doing reflexive anthropology entails more than just reflecting on our

privilege; it demands that we engage the emotions and participate in the interrogations sparked by these exchanges.[4]

Guilt and Catharsis

No matter how much the ethnographer prepares, interviews rarely go as planned.
What is discussed and how the conversation develops are often unpredictable.
After the fact, feelings of frustration and dissatisfaction are common. On rare
occasions, however, an interview turns into something truly amazing: an opportunity not only to ask questions but also to discuss bigger issues. At these times,
emotional intensity runs high, possibilities open up, and the interview exceeds
all expectations. I remember two such occasions: one in Veracruz, Mexico, and
the other in La Paz, Bolivia.

Sorcery was central to the experience in Veracruz. In Latin America, sorcery
is a form of symbolic violence. It is an aggressive action, but it is also defensive,
a way of channeling violence in subdued and oppressed sectors, in areas where
the upper echelons of society monopolize violence. In Veracruz, sorcery is a
defensive response to aggression and social domination. My encounter with
Juanos, a gay tailor, was connected to sorcery. We were introduced at a gradua-
tion party where I was identified as a "Spanish friend." I recalled the encounter
in my field notes:

> When I shook his hand, Juanos stumbled, pushing my hand toward me, and for
> some 8 or 10 seconds we engaged in a kind of vertical arm wrestling contest. Then
> he let go (I wasn't pressing his hand one bit), angrily leaving me to sit back in
> his chair. At that point, all the guys sitting at my table stood up to ask me what
> had happened. When I told them, they expressed disbelief and disgust. They
> exclaimed in loud voices, "Hey, what was that!" "Ugh!" and "What's wrong with
> that faggot!" They joked about him being gay, inferring that by shaking my hand
> he had gotten so excited [he] couldn't control himself. One even said, "he got such
> a thrill from that he shit his pants!" (Diary, November 22, 1996)

Obviously my initial encounter with Juanos had not gone all that well. Yet I
still wanted to get to know him. Thanks to the mediation of friends, we were
soon able to meet again. Making a visit to his workshop-house, I recorded what
Juanos said to me:

Look, I'm sorry for the other day but you really brought me down and I wasn't even that drunk. On top of that, I was with a friend who is kind of obnoxious and after he saw you and I struggle, he slapped me and said, "What's your problem?" I don't know what came over me but for some reason I was scared. I guess it may have been because I didn't know you yet felt you were full of vibes . . . Yes, that's exactly what happened! you were loaded with vibes, but were not aware, or were you? . . . No, you exuded those vibes and you let that energy loose. It was an energy picked up from all those people you have visited lately. I don't know if it is a negative or positive vibe [between us]. It's probably positive cause we haven't done anything wrong, have we? (Interview, November 25, 1996)

He placed what had happened between us in relation to what he had heard about my research with some of the Veracruz *spiritual science* mediums. In shaking hands with me, he figured that I had transmitted negative "vibes" "accumulated" during my ethnographic fieldwork.

I came to learn that Juanos had worked on several occasions for Spanish businessmen. Our encounter was colored for him by these negative experiences. He told me of a traumatic experience while working as an accountant. On one occasion, he got in serious trouble for stealing. He tried to justify this theft by claiming that Spaniards living in Veracruz were exploitative, arrogant, and rude. Sometimes, he figured, they even broke the law. When Juanos got caught embezzling money, his boss held him prisoner. Kept in the cellar of a warehouse, Juanos was interrogated and beaten. Unable to make him confess, the Spaniard turned him over to the Veracruz municipal police, who threw him in jail. Two days later, a friend who was a lawyer was able to get him released. Juanos stole from another Spanish employer as well. When he was discovered, Juanos sought refuge in a ranch in Tilapa, near San Andres Tuxtla in southern Veracruz. To "distract" his boss, he relied on dark sorcery: he "sent" an illness to one of his boss's close relatives to keep the boss from pursuing him. Until I heard Juanos's testimony, I had known nothing about his previous negative experiences with other Spaniards. Nor did I realize the extent that he was into magic and spiritualism. When friends introduced me as being from Spain, Juanos's conflicted history with his Spanish employers clearly sparked a strong reaction in him. As ethnographers, we understand that our positionality will influence our relationships with key interlocutors. It may block access to certain information, people, and places. It may cause people to resist, even violently reject us. Overcoming these roadblocks may necessitate measures that spark an emotional catharsis. For Juanos, I "stood in" for someone from his past. Our interaction was cathartic because it helped him work through a personal trauma.

What happens when we encounter someone who has experienced intense trauma? In late September 2002 in La Paz, Bolivia, I was introduced to Dr. Marco Antonio A. by Dr. Jorge Molina, director of the Hospital Sagrado Corazón de Jesús (Kenko) up in the Alto (a highland district). Marco Antonio had worked as a pediatrician in that same hospital as well as in the nearby Hospital Boliviano Español. His was an extended "provincial" service period that ran two years, twice as long as mandated. While we were sitting comfortably in a downtown hotel lobby, I asked him to tell me a little about his compulsory internship working in the countryside during the early 1990s.[5] His first appointment was at the hospital of Huancoyo followed by a stint at the Tiahuanaco medical center and then a six-month stay in the relatively isolated village of Amarete. He recalled his internship in quite an emotional way. I noted the following:

> Yesterday's intensity and especially my interview with Marco Antonio, has increased my tension level. The interview lasted for over two hours. It took place in the lobby of the Prado Hotel where we had a couple of "Old Parr" whiskies. The drinks eased the doctor's account, opening wounds associated [with] his experiences during his rural internship in the northwestern rural town of Amarete [near the Peruvian border]. (Diary, October 1, 2002)

Marco Antonio shared that during his residency in Amarete, locals expressed minimal interest in the kind of Western medicine he had to offer. He feared that the scant number of patients whom he treated cast him in more of a social than a medical role:

> I didn't have many consultations. On good days I counted seven, eight, maybe ten. But a doctor with such a little amount of work is not really practicing medicine, right? I mostly spoke to the people, about their problems, they told me about the harvest, about their current needs: they wanted money, or to travel to the city, to send their kids to the city, to learn and drive a car, so they may return with a truck. That's their big dream. But I didn't see a lot of interest in my medical expertise. (Interview, September 30, 2002)

When Marco Antonio moved to the village of Amarete, things got worse with the arrival of the French Friends of Amarete, an NGO. Negotiating with the French volunteers, Marco Antonio agreed to cook for the NGO in exchange for food. A while later, he contracted pneumonia. Neither the Bolivian Ministry of Health nor members of the French NGO were willing to help. His life at risk, Marco Antonio was treated by Don Fernando, a Kallawaya traditional healer:

> Don Fernando had treated me like a servant, until I got ill. I had pneumonia, pneumonia. . . . I was scared, I was so scared that I thought I had tuberculosis. Shit! I thought I had tuberculosis because I started coughing, and blood came out of my mouth. "Shit! It's tuberculosis, it's tuberculosis . . . !" So, instead of helping me, they ignored me. They have messed up my life! Living in Amarete has been horrible! Fernando was the only person, because those guys in the NGO I told you about, they didn't do anything, they didn't even intervene: "Are you sick? Oh, take him to La Paz!" "Do we take him by car?" "Oh no, we don't have gas!" Motherfuckers! I was laying around, sick. . . . Then Don Fernando did something I never expected. He started preparing some medicines. He started working on me, he had some sophisticated tricks. He made ointments, containers, using eucalyptus, pine, cedar, chamomile, which are elements commonly used for preparing ointments. He started one day, when I was already burning with fever, I was feeling terrible. First, there wasn't anyone to cook for me. I wasn't hungry at all, anyway. Then Fernando came with some soup, I didn't know its ingredients but do you know what he put in it? He had gotten up early, very early, gone to the river and caught a couple of trout. He made a soup with one and roasted the other. Who knew? He comes to me and says, "eat this, come on . . . !" And then he said something I will never forget, "If you don't eat, you're going to die!" I didn't want to die and was terrified. (Interview, September 30, 2002)

With his natural medicine and treatments, Don Fernando slowly began to nurse Marco Antonio back to health.

> [After a while] my fever went down and I fell asleep. I didn't wake up for about a whole day. . . . And, wow! I woke up feeling much better. The old man had been near my bedside. "Food, eat," he said. I was hungry so I did. But soon he told me, "You are still not well, you have to leave Amarete." Then he said, "Marco, people here don't like you, they have bewitched you." I didn't agree. I thought I had gotten sick because I smoked a lot and ate very little. I had not been sleeping much. But he insisted, "No, you have been enchanted. So, in order for you to get better, I have to heal you. In order to heal you we are going to my house." Shit, once we

got to his hut, he started making a cloud of smoke with his herbs! And he gave me some sticks, strong stuff! The old man almost killed me! Don Fernando was performing an exorcism on me, trying to dissipate my disease. Once I came to my senses I shouted, "What is this? What are you doing?" Then I realized what I had gotten myself into. Oh my God! Amarete is place of sorcery . . . a damn cradle of sorcery, witchdoctors all! (Interview, September 30, 2002)

It appeared as if not only Don Fernando but the people of the village had turned against Marco Antonio. Did they not appreciate his sacrifice? Was his medical training no longer welcome?

Marco Antonio gradually recovered from his illness. He continued his work, however undervalued, for a few more months before again facing a difficult challenge. This time, a handful of Amarete residents actually requested that Marco Antonio leave the village. They wanted to convert the modest clinic where he was working into a residential dormitory for teachers. Once again, Marco Antonio found himself without support from the Bolivian authorities. Not wanting to leave his practice, he was able to negotiate a compromise with the local authorities. In exchange for turning over the hospital, he would be allowed two rooms—one to be his living quarters and the other to treat his patients. This agreement was reached only after the doctor also agreed, in no doubt a somewhat humiliating gesture, to become the building's "caretaker." The tension between himself and village residents was palpable in his retelling. Fear and misunderstanding ran high on both sides. Shockingly, the doctor even shared with me his belief that the townspeople might have wanted to go so far as to lynch him.

When I later published my account of the doctor's difficult situation in the Bolivian backcountry, I expressed my deep gratitude. I wrote in my acknowledgments, "To Doctor Marco Antonio A. for opening up the scars and the dignity of his trade." The fine whiskey that we shared might have stimulated the personal revelations that day in the Prado Hotel. However, the alcohol was not solely responsible for making Marco Antonio vulnerable to an ethnographer: he also had agency here. By sharing his excruciating trial as a budding professional, Marco Antonio reaffirmed his own ability to take on some of life's most difficult challenges and survive.

The etymology of catharsis signals the expiation of guilt or bodily purging or cleansing. For Juanos, guilt for stealing from his Spanish employers and causing them pain cannot be divorced from the trauma and humiliation caused by their abusive behavior. For Marco Antonio, guilt over not being able to treat patients in Amarete was associated with feelings of abandonment and the fear of death. In both cases, guilt festered until our conversations allowed them to relive these feelings. For Juanos, he came to associate this guilt with me due to my Spanish background, but through my gentle and friendly questioning, he experienced a catharsis. As I listened to these stories, I shared this feeling of catharsis because I became emotionally invested in their pain. Their reliving of the emotions attached to these acts of suffering transformed them, but they also transformed me.

Dreams and Fears

Carlos Castañeda (2000) in *The Teachings of Don Juan* suggests that dreams should be taken seriously in ethnographic inquiry because they reveal spiritual knowledge and signal structural relations of power. As such, dreams can serve as epistemological and methodological tools for field research. I suggest that dreams are another type of journeying that remains unexplored in critical reflections of travel and tourism. The act of writing down one's dreams during field experience makes it possible for us to explore how social immersion impacts our consciousness. Even before we begin fieldwork, anticipatory dreams about one's place of research can help prepare us emotionally and psychologically for travel. Yet our dreams are rarely factored into scholarly writings. Dreams can be interpreted as another type of "travel," less Cartesian and physical. Even daydreams, memories, or visions can be interpreted in a similar fashion.[6] These types of "travels," to a large extent, modulate, match up with, and mold the reality of our travails.

Although we are familiar with psychological and psychoanalytic analysis of dreams, sociological and anthropological perspectives offer another approach.[7] By focusing on the sociocultural connections and patterns of dreams in different cultures,[8] we can use dreams as another analytical tool to understand our field experience.[9] Writing down my dreams has allowed me to explore modes of communication, subjectivities, and processes of assimilation. By converting dreams into discourse and narrative text, we can explore processes of cross-cultural identification and "immersion." As we analyze our dreams, we become the subjects of study. In "The Ethnographer," Jorge Luis Borges (1974) posits dreams as central to fieldwork and as catalysts for knowledge production.

A few weeks before traveling to Mexico for the first time in 1989, I had a vivid dream. Writing in my diary upon awaking, I named my entry, "Portrait of an eerie and terrifying dream." Somewhat anxious about the new world I was about to encounter, I found condensed in this dream all my fears and insecurities about living in Veracruz:

> Going down a mountain highway on a dark gray day, I approached a turn when I heard a loud crash. I saw ahead that the road was blocked by two smoking vehicles which had just collided. I looked up at the rocks and sharp cliffs in front of me and I saw a series of balconies made of wood with small windows. Above these are flying vultures (or maybe eagles) that are making heartrending screams. I realize a man and a woman are on one of these balconies. The man is lying down on what appears to be [a] stretcher or maybe even an open coffin while the woman is trying to cover him so the vultures won't eat him. The scene was very odd and I found it terrifying. (Diary, April 22, 1989)

Despite it being quite a strange dream, I did not think much about it.

Over the next few years while living in Veracruz, I continued to keep a diary of my experience—both waking and otherwise—as I established a relationship with the city and its people. Veracruz is a place where countless stories about bodily and sexual excess have become a central part of the local identity. Not surprisingly, this intimate discourse entered my imagination and my investigative practices. A good part of my written notes manifest sexual, even scatological, themes. The visions or experiences that I discuss below can be understood as an extreme kind of the *altered perception* that James Davies (2010, 94–95) identifies as a persistent emotion or state characterizing the situation of fieldwork.

At one point after a long Veracruz night, I had an extraordinary experience that existed somewhere between wakefulness and dreaming.[10] I wrote it down in my diary:

> From the roof terrace in the house on Rincón de la Trova, around 4:30 or 5 am, I was lying down without my glasses, waiting for someone to bring me a bottle of water while being terribly thirsty (I hadn't drunk alcohol). I felt exhausted and somewhat cold as I looked at a vacant office building in front of me and the waning moon above. The moon had a beautiful halo of light around it. I felt relaxed and could hear the sounds of the birds and bats about the terrace. Suddenly I saw

something moving in front of me. At first it appeared to be a bird but then it looked more like piece of paper or silk floating capriciously in the air. [As it was] caught in the light of the moon, I thought I saw it briefly in the shape of a small skeleton, the lines of its bones clearly marked and having a small skull of a cat on top. The image deeply frightened me for some reason as I saw [it] gradually being carried off by the wind. (Diary, September 8, 1993)

I felt scared and helpless in the presence of that cat's skeleton floating through the air! I thought of it bringing harm to its destination, perhaps some kind of bad luck to someone south of the city, where some of my friends and their families lived.

I remember telling my friend George and his mother, doña Mari, about this "vision." It impressed them, and they later asked me about it several times. They thought that the vision had something to do with my work interviewing people closely connected to the spiritual world. Both knew that I had been in contact with some individuals who practiced Trinitarian Marian spiritualism, which included the practice of sorcery and the sending of "harms." George and doña Mari considered the vision to be a sign of immersion in and comprehension of the spiritualist beliefs and practices of Veracruz. They suggested that the floating cat skeleton reflected my empathy for the "victims" who were touched by sorcery. When I heard this, I felt a deep sense of acceptance and respect. Perhaps the vision was a sign of my successfully being integrated—at least to some degree—into the culture of Veracruz?

When I traveled to Bolivia in fall 2002, I experienced a powerful sense of déjà vu. As we descended from the highlands to downtown La Paz, I thought that I recognized the landscape, the constructions, and neighborhoods from a dream some years before. There were some of the same house balconies on sharp cliffs. The fear and anxiety that had infiltrated my dream in 1993 resurfaced. When I arrived at the hotel, I wrote in my journal: "Look for a record of this dream in travel diaries 1989–1993." I then elaborated:

I can't help but feel impressed by many things here in Bolivia: the extreme dryness, the lack of trees and the dust in the air. [Like in the dream I had before going to Mexico] the houses appear to be hanging from the slopes of the mountain valley where La Paz is located. It reminds me of the deserted landscape in my dream where the couple appeared to be living in a cage, like birds, hanging from the mountain walls. Those same images that came to me in a dream in 1989 before my visit to Mexico now seem to have come to life while cruising down the highway here in Bolivia! At this moment, I shuddered, contemplating the notion that after more than a decade I was now living in [my] former dreamscape in all its intensity and beauty. (Diary, September 17, 2002)

By keeping a journal of dreams that I had during my research, I was able to reconnect with experiences from the past and with the emotions that had shaped that past. In this specific instance, this sense of a corporeal geography of travel took place at a critical period in my own career, in which I was anticipating entry into a new and different culture under a different circumstance. My awareness of this transition had taken shape not just in my conscious mind but also in my subconscious memory and dreaming self.

Coda

With the hindsight of twenty-five years of investigations and returns, I acknowledge that my interpretation of the conversations and emotions that I shared here matters beyond the texts that I have produced. In deliberating on the corporeal, intimate, and subjective, we challenge disciplinary boundaries and hegemonic and occidental representations. However, as a scholar working in a European institution, I am implicated in these asymmetric power relations. By exposing the intimate fragments of field research—my doubts and emotions— and by sharing personal encounters that I have not previously divulged, I reposition traditional ethnographic methods that determine who is the authority and who can ask questions.

Fernando Giobellina (2003, 25) reminds us that fieldwork is immersive. As such, it can lead to a dissociative state that we feel through our bodies:

> When "in the field," the researcher experiences otherness in his own flesh. The socialization of networks of rules, values, and interpretative categories he undergoes, the forced assimilation of alien disciplines that compromise not only his conduct but his body (eating, sleeping, and moving around with others, as others), lead to—at least in my case—a decentralization from one's own culture. After some time, the person engaged in fieldwork no longer belongs to his place of origin, as well as to his place of work: he does not belong anywhere. He is not a representative of his culture, but, to a great extent, an exile.

Fieldwork, through its in-between existence, can transform us into different people. Sharing these profound personal, intimate, affective, and corporeal changes should be central to our methods and narration (Gutiérrez and Surrallés 2015, 15–16). Rather than considering subjectivity to have a corrosive and negative effect in the field, I treat emotions—or *embodied thoughts* as defined by Michelle Zimbalist Rosaldo (1984)—as central to knowledge production, ethnographic inquiry, and the act of writing. Emotions are an epistemological and methodological component central to the field, like analysis, reflection, and writing an anthropological text. Through a focus on emotions and their manifestations in everyday encounters, global imaginaries, personal interrogations, and dreams, I contend that an "affective turn" in anthropological inquiry is just as necessary as a "reflective turn."

Notes

1. I have been working for some years on developing an emotional anthropological perspective. See Flores 2010, 2015; Flores and Díaz 2010.
2. The DGCP is a national organization involved in the promotion, conservation, and development of Mexican Indigenous popular culture.
3. I thank M. Bianet Castellanos for pointing out the connection between memory and ethnography.
4. See Clifford 1990, 1999; Graburn 1977; Flores 2010.
5. *Año de provincias* is how Bolivian people call the compulsory rural service demanded of medical graduates—as well as of graduates in such fields as nursing and dentistry. It is a period of unpaid service carried out in rural areas (Flores 2004, 183).
6. I have written an essay on the spiritual trips of my interlocutors. See Flores 2000.
7. See Von Grunebaum and Callois 1966; Bastide 1966.
8. See Tedlock 1992; Mageo 2003.
9. See Zivkovic 2006; Tobón 2015.
10. *Extraordinary experience* or *anomalous experience* is how some authors (Young and Goulet 1994; McClenon and Nooney 2002; Goulet and Miller 2007) have recently referred to certain encounters or situations in fieldwork; these experiences can hardly be definitively labeled as wakefulness or dream, or be interpreted from a Cartesian, rational viewpoint.

References

Bastide, Roger. 1966. "The Sociology of the Dream." In *The Dream and Human Societies*, edited by Gustave E. Von Grunebaum and Roger Callois, 199–211. Berkeley: University of California Press.

Borges, Jorge Luis. 1974. "The Ethnographer." In *In Praise of Darkness*, 46–51. New York: E. P. Dutton.

Bourdieu, Pierre. 1999. *The Weight of the World: Social Suffering in Contemporary Society*. Stanford, Calif.: Stanford University Press.

Castañeda, Carlos. 2000. *The Teachings of Don Juan: A Yaqui Way of Knowledge*. New York: Washington Square Press.

Clifford, James. 1990. "Notes on (Field)notes." In *Fieldnotes: The Making of Anthropology*, edited by Rojer Sanjek, 47–70. Cornell, N.Y.: Cornell University Press.

Clifford, James. 1999. Prácticas espaciales: El trabajo de campo, el viaje y la disciplina de la antropología. In *Itinerarios transculturales*, 71–119. Barcelona: Gedisa.

Davies, James. 2010. "Disorientation, Dissonance and Altered Perception in the Field." In Davies and Spencer 2010, 79–97.

Davies, James, and Dimitrina Spencer, eds. 2010. *Emotions in the Field: The Psychology and Anthropology of Fieldwork Experience*. Stanford, Calif.: Stanford University Press.

Flores, Juan Antonio. 2000. "Viajes espirituales en el Puerto de Veracruz (México)." *Cuadernos Hispanoamericanos* 597:43–53.

Flores, Juan Antonio. 2004. "Una etnografía del 'año de provincias' y de 'cuando no hay doctor.'" In *Salud e Interculturalidad en América Latina. Perspectivas Antropológicas*, edited by Gerardo Fernandez Juárez, 181–212. Quito, Ecuador: Abya-Yala.

Flores, Juan Antonio. 2010. "Trabajo de campo etnográfico y gestión emocional: Notas epistemológicas y metodológicas." *Ankulegi: Revista de Antropología Social* 14:11–23.

Flores, Juan Antonio. 2015. "Paseos y tránsitos emocionales en Veracruz. Una etnografía de agencias espirituales y clubes anónimos de autoayuda." In *Retórica de los sentimientos. Etnografías amerindias*, edited by Manuel Gutéirrez and Alexandre Surrallés, 233–64. Madrid: Editorial Iberoamericana-Vervuert.

Flores, Juan Antonio, and Rafael Díaz. 2010. "Emociones en el etnógrafo: Equipaje y destrezas difíciles en el campo y la escritura." In *Emociones y sentimientos: Enfoques interdisciplinares*, edited by Luisa Abad and Juan Antonio Flores, 95–123. Cuenca, Ecuador: Ediciones de la Universidad de Castilla-La Mancha.

Frohlick, Susan. 2013. "Intimate Tourism Markets: Money, Gender, and the Complexity of Erotic Exchange in a Costa Rican Caribbean Town." *Anthropological Quarterly* 86 (1): 133–62.

Giobellina, Fernando. 2003. *Sentidos de la Antropología, Antropología de los Sentidos*. Cádiz, Spain: Servicio de Publicaciones de la Universidad de Cádiz.

Goulet, Jean-Guy, and Bruce G. Miller, eds. 2007. *Extraordinary Anthropology: Transformations in the Field*. Lincoln: University of Nebraska Press.

Graburn, Nelson H. H. 1977. "Tourism: The Sacred Journey." In *Hosts and Guests: The Anthropology of Tourism*, edited by Valene Smith, 17–31. Philadelphia: University of Pennsylvania Press.

Gutiérrez, Manuel, and Alexandre Surrallés, eds. 2015. *Retórica de los sentimientos. Etnografías amerindias*. Madrid: Editorial Iberoamericana-Vervuert.

Harrison, Julia. 2003. *Being a Tourist: Finding Meaning in Pleasure Travel*. Vancouver: University of British Columbia Press.

Lai, Paul, and Lindsey Claire Smith, eds. 2010. "Introduction." *American Quarterly* 62 (3): 407–36.

Mageo, Jeannette M., ed. 2003. *Dreaming and the Self: New Perspectives on Subjectivity, Identity, and Emotion*. Albany: State University of New York Press.

McClenon, James, and Jennifer Nooney. 2002. "Anomalous Experiences Reported by Field Anthropologists: Evaluating Theories Regarding Religion." *Anthropology of Consciousness* 13 (2): 46–60.

Rosaldo, Michelle Zimbalist. 1984. "Toward an Anthropology of Self and Feeling." In *Culture Theory: Essays on Mind, Self, and Emotion*, edited by Richard A. Shweder and Robert A. LeVine, 137–57. Cambridge: Cambridge University Press.

Rulfo, Juan. (1955) 1994. *Pedro Páramo*. New York: Grove Press.

Sacramento, Octávio. 2017. "'Mulé' tem que ficar esperta: Turismo, encontros passionais e gestão feminina da intimidade no nordeste do Brasil." *Mana* 23 (1): 137–65.

Salazar, Noel B. 2010. *Envisioning Eden: Mobilizing Imaginaries in Tourism and Beyond*. Oxford: Berghahn.

Tedlock, Barbara, ed. 1992. *Dreaming: Anthropological and Psychological Interpretations*. Santa Fe, N.Mex.: School of American Research Press.

Tobón, Marco. 2015. "Los sueños como instrumentos etnográficos." *AIBR: Revista de Antropología Iberoamericana* 10 (3): 331–53.

Von Grunebaum, Gustave, and Roger Callois, eds. 1966. *The Dream and Human Societies*. Berkeley: University of California Press.

Young, David E., and Jean-Guy Goulet, eds. 1994. *Being Changed by Cross-Cultural Encounters: The Anthropology of Extraordinary Experience*. Ontario: Broadview Press.

Zivkovic, Marko. 2006. "Sueños dentro-fuera: Algunos usos del sueño en la teoría social y la investigación etnográfica." *Revista de Antropología Social* 15:139–71.

THREE

La Quebrada

A Foreign Journalist Takes the Plunge

BARBARA KASTELEIN

I moved to Mexico in summer 1995, not as an anthropologist or historian but as a recent PhD in popular culture and literature, joining a handsome man (intriguingly, an astrologer) whom I had met in April while visiting friends. Soon after, I took a job as a copyeditor with a new English-language newspaper called the *Mexico City Times*. My friends had made me some introductions, which had opened up the possibility of work as a lecturer in the capital's giant state university, the National Autonomous University of Mexico, known as "la UNAM." But I knew that this lectureship would pay poorly, and I was wary of the insularity of academic life after experiencing a depression when completing my postgraduate studies, which I ascribed to feeling isolated from the "real" world and the healthy dynamics of teamwork. No more dry abstractions and torturous self-referential thought for me: I was after more verifiable and tangible "truths."

So I tried new waters, journalism. While my boyfriend related the symbols of the zodiac to daily life, I learned about news reporting as a way to get my teeth into my adopted country. This was a fraught time for Mexico, following the assassination of presidential candidate Luis Donaldo Colosio in March 1994. But the moment was also dynamic, politically and socially, and the characters and their antics in the news, so outlandish to my way of thinking, baffled and thrilled me. The country was in the throes of the Zapatista uprising and the implementation of NAFTA, and the atmosphere—pregnant with a colorful tumult of tradition, revolution, and resistance—felt strangely optimistic and edgy. Or it certainly did by phlegmatic British standards. A series of changes was underway that would lead five years later to the country's first democratically elected government, and the very street corners in Mexico City seemed to burst with energy. The morning air, blending the smells of makeshift stalls with tidal waves of belching traffic, shimmered and hiccupped with expectation.

Although we lived in the capital, I passed through Acapulco as often as I could, usually on my way with my boyfriend to stay for a long weekend at a rustic cliff-top cabin owned by his mother in Pie de la Cuesta, just a few miles up the coast. My heart always skipped a beat at the first sight of the glittering blue and silver bay spread before us, as we finally left the highway dust and the ominous sierra behind. To me Acapulco meant tropical romance and glamour, even if by the 1990s it had become tawdry and acquired some sordid undertones. Was it that I had known of the Acapulco cliff divers since I was eight years old, when I first watched the Elvis Presley movie *Fun in Acapulco*? My dad, whom I adored at that age (it was he who taught me "rester, c'est exister, voyager, c'est vivre"), was the oracle. He had at that time told me that Acapulco was a real place, that the cliff diving at the end of the movie took place in real life, and that the Acapulco cliff divers were courageous and skillful men. Whatever the reason, I, like others of my generation and a little older, had grown up with a sense of Acapulco as the ultimate tropical holiday destination; if one could travel for the sake of pure delight, Acapulco would be the mecca. Furthermore, Acapulco—"the Pearl of the Pacific," "the Queen of the Mexican Riviera," as it used to be called—was the meeting place of reality and glamour. Everybody had heard of it and knew it was paradise. It brought someone normal like me into contact with glitzy fame, the sing-along world of Elvis, a Technicolor promised land of romance and laughter beneath the waving palms.

Not only could Acapulco bring someone romantic, as I am, into contact with the luxury and legends of the past, but it might validate my "mad" decision to leave the United Kingdom.

For I did so just as my academic career was starting and my friends were settling down and having children. I uprooted myself and discarded my past—as my parents had done, from the Netherlands to England, in October 1966, when I was three months old. The Calvinistic parents of my mother, then a young nurse, had disapproved of my father, seventeen years her senior and very bohemian, having spent most of his twenties and thirties traveling with a guitar on his back. Not only had my parents virtually eloped for their wedding—which

was only scantly attended by the huge Dutch families of either side—but when
my dad was called back to Holland by his job at Phillips in his early forties,
they decided to stay in England, on no funds, for him to retrain as a language
teacher. Ironically, they did not teach me Dutch, my native tongue, stranding me
in the British Isles. Exposed very early to my father's taste for "cowboy films," I
saw Mexico as a place of bad guys and lawlessness, but also of risk and escape. I
chose to learn Spanish instead of German at my UK school, partly in defiance of
the notion that I should be good at German because I was Dutch, partly because
it seemed a romantic language and I had seen a television documentary that
showed how widely spoken it was in the wider "world," meaning the Americas.

* * *

I first started writing about Acapulco in 2003 as a freelance travel writer in
an article for the *Scotsman* newspaper, to which my editor gave the title "It's a
Dive but I Love It." My growing partiality and preferred theme were to develop
later in my travel column in such articles as "Saving Acapulco's Golden Age,"
but putting aside for a moment my urge to rescue Acapulco and rediscover, for
myself and my readers, its faded beauty and allure, the bottom line was that I
had to sell these articles to pay my way. I had to cover my costs when in Acapulco and justify the time I spent on it.

My first foray into writing about the world-famous cliff divers came thanks
to three interviews that I held with veteran divers at the end of 2004 for a
chapter of a book, *Holiday in Mexico* (Wood and Berger 2009), which would
address tourism in Mexico from an anthropological and historical point of view.
My task was to look at "denial and contemporary mythmaking" in Acapulco—
how service providers in the tourism industry tried to pretend that time had
not passed and that the resort had not declined from its glory days of the late
1950s to the mid-1970s. But I had a hidden agenda, one that was not fully conscious to me but that was evident in the high levels of nervous excitement with
which I approached my interviewees. At that point, I had lived in Mexico as a
journalist and travel writer for nearly seven years (so I was no longer a tourist
in Mexico, although I was one in Acapulco) and I rarely felt so elated when I
met the subjects of my stories. What was different?

One of the divers, Antonio Velazquez, boasted about his and his colleagues'
amorous conquests with women of both dark and light skin, and he made a
fanciful comparison of me to Brigitte Bardot, whom he had met during the

divers' glory days. His flirtatious banter charmed me. Another told me, "We are just part of Acapulco's yesterday," which moved me because I was by then a fan of the resort and dedicated to finding remnants of its dazzling past. This was all the more poignant because I knew that Acapulco's fortunes had suffered dramatically when it was eclipsed by the creation of Cancún in the mid-1970s. I felt that the cliff divers and Acapulco were so much more than just part of yesterday. But it was Ignacio Sánchez, known as Nacho, who gave me the idea of writing a book about the Acapulco cliff divers, with his solemn account of the divers' history—stretching as far back as 1934 (I had assumed that they dated to the 1950s)—and their wages, injuries, and feats, including performances abroad. My first question after our lengthy interview was whether a book had been written, and he said no, that some had tried but with no result (many of the older cliff divers had limited schooling and struggled with literacy). He also directed me to a woman called Myrna who was the widow of Raúl "Chupetas" García, a former leader of the cliff-diving union who had been friends with Frank Sinatra and who had been responsible for bringing the divers into contact with Hollywood.

One topic that Nacho didn't encourage me to pursue was my interest in a young girl diver whom I had seen perform in August 2004. My journalist antennae were alerted by this beautiful child who was coached in climbing halfway up the cliff face by her father, and who did a perfect dive from a height around eighteen meters (fifty-nine feet) into the chasm of churning waves. But Nacho let me believe that this event was, if not an aberration, then certainly an exception to the rule, and he said that if I was serious about Acapulco's traditions and the history of the cliff divers, I should turn my interest elsewhere. I did as he suggested, interviewing Myrna six months later, and her story about her departed husband encouraged me further in the idea for a book. The man was clearly a legend, and I was shocked to hear that not even one proper obituary had been written about him. I also, almost surreptitiously, interviewed Iris, the girl diver, and published an article about her in December 2005 in the *Observer*. This article proved my hunch that I had landed on a great story, as I received over forty emails of inquiry about the girl the day after publication, even from *Guinness World Records* and Italy's *Vogue*!

I decided to test the waters for my book idea with a feature article in Spanish in the magazine *Gato Pardo*, and the topic I chose was the cliff divers' reputations as Latin lovers. By that time Antonio had suffered a stroke and was less boastful and more candid about his experiences, including about those with women tourists who were interested in his services as a gigolo. I found that my

personal estimation of the divers and respect for their world conflicted with
the journalist in me who wanted the juiciest story. The former won, and I did
not include Antonio's tale about the women who left him money (or the one
who was going to share her fortune with him and had sent him a passport so
he could join her in the United States, which he finally refused to do because
his wife in Acapulco was pregnant and "I wanted to know my own blood," he
said). But I did include a comment from a waitress who knew the cliff divers
well, which was that she knew Nacho's "real wife," meaning the first woman
with whom he had had children. That I printed this comment, Nacho told me,
upset his current partner, with whom he had a seven-year-old son. I also took a
risk and mentioned the marriage of another cliff diver, Ricardo Vega, to French
adventuress and nightclub entrepreneur Jaqueline Petite, with whom he had a
daughter, although Jaqueline said that she would deny "everything" if I mentioned Ricardo in connection with her.

I was aware that the theme of my article was slightly risqué, deliberately so
as I wanted to whet readers' appetites and see what kind of tales would arise. I
was not aware of how the article would reflect on me, sexualizing me as a white
woman "from" England who was asking about love affairs and awakening slum-
bering histories of escapades with foreign women. It turned out that Raúl "Chupetas" García, as I heard from Myrna, also had children abroad who had grown
up with their foreign mothers and who barely knew their cliff-diver father.[1]
Instinctively I tended to keep to myself and was shy of asking the younger
divers about their encounters—especially as when I met them, they were nearly
always wearing nothing but their swimming trunks. From their point of view I
was another foreign woman who "wanted a piece." I might not have been one
of the American war widows who found their gigolos here, but nevertheless I
was seeking stories and an opportunity to pen "their" book.

I soon formulated my investigations as a "help" to the divers as my articles
brought positive publicity, something that Acapulco needed. But I was ignoring
a subtlety: the divers were not synonymous with Acapulco, and they had an
ambivalent relationship with Acapulco's tourism authorities, who bristled at the
divers' independence and insistence on doing things in their own way. Years later
I found that another woman from England, called Tina, had done something
similar in helping the divers with their public relations, but she had married a
cliff diver and was thus more immersed in the scene than I was, although she
was less experienced in journalism.

The divers gave my assistance a cool welcome; they were curious at articles, especially the photos, but they were not eager to organize all the press clippings in a file, which is what I would have done. The article about the cliff-diver girl led to my help getting Iris in *Guinness World Records*, but the text was altered from my article. Whereas I had said that she was the "only chica" in the cliff-diver scene, the record book claimed that she was "the youngest person—and first female" to dive from eighteen meters (Guinness World Records 2007, 508). This statement was not wholly true as Ricardo Vega had a son who had done that dive at the age of eight. To Ricardo I was "la culpable del Records Guinness"—the guilty one. "Why wasn't *my* son in *Guinness World Records*?" Ricardo asked me angrily, to which I wanted to say that I had not been there at the time to help with publicity. But that was not the point that he wanted to make. His point was that the text that had been published as a result of my article contained an inaccuracy, and I was the one who should be held to account. My view at the time was that the divers should be glad of something that in fact did later lead to more fabulous publicity, a documentary with the Discovery Channel.[2] It hadn't occurred to me that I might be upsetting the apple cart of hierarchies in the diver community by emphasizing the feats of Iris Alvarez, and therefore tipping the balance toward the Alvarez clan. It cost me great effort and my pride to realize that I was expecting gratitude and a deeper welcome when, from another point of view, I had meddled and more or less told a lie.[3] So much for the "tangible truths" of journalism.

* * *

By 2004, I was established as a travel writer, spoke the same language as the tourism departments and promoters (in addition to a competent Spanish), and had begun to grasp my worth as someone who could generate much-needed publicity. I read as much as I could about the anthropology of tourism and tried to fine-tune my awareness of power relations in host and guest interactions. After all, this topic was something that had long interested me: first with concern for the ways that these power relations warped the cultural and emotional experience of "authentic difference" and the broadening of the mind that I sincerely believed travel should offer, and second, when I became more jaded, with an eye on the ways that these power imbalances could be put to comically disconcerting effect in narrative.

But in my eagerness to be midwife to Acapulco's renaissance, especially through the memories and high-octane experiences of the cliff divers, I forgot to examine my own tricks of the trade as a reporter—my unusual ability to move around, gain access, engage different classes of people in conversation, and win confidences—which by then were second nature to me. I was good at finding just the right interviewee and persisting until I got the interview, and I had a knack for eliciting punchy quotations. Yet these successes were not because I was a good anthropologist but because I was a reporter. I had been shy as a child and a teen, and my work as a reporter had helped me grow the thicker skin necessary to overcome ordinary inhibitions and stray out of my comfort zone, shift my world away from "home," and explore beautiful and exotic, and slightly scary, places.

My first major faux pas with a cliff diver took place in my very first interview, with Nacho (Ignacio Sánchez), the former champion who was then fifty-seven years old. We were drinking a Coke in a taco joint across the plaza from where the public can buy tickets for the dive show. A gulf opened up between us along the fault-line of media publicity—more precisely Elvis Presley and Hollywood glamour. I had asked Nacho what he remembered of filming with Elvis and received a dark look that took me quite aback. "Elvis nunca estuvo aquí" (Elvis was never here). For a moment my brain went on freeze, as though Nacho had said that water isn't wet. But I felt the smile sliding off my face before the vehemence of his stare. "If you will forgive the impropriety," he said courteously, while lowering his gaze, "Elvis said he would rather be with a dog on a street than with a Mexican woman. That is why he was not welcome."

I was completely unprepared for this. The First World, Eurocentric media hound in me had assumed that Elvis, "the King," could only have been good news for the cliff divers. I expected to hear something about how Elvis was not really diving from the high cliff, and some information on who had doubled him on screen. But "dog on a street"! The racial insult to a Mexican woman, and also Nacho's thoughtful manners in apologizing to me for what he was about to repeat, whirled around in a maelstrom of power imbalance and embarrassment. Nacho, a senior gentleman from a southern state in Mexico, apologized to *me*, a white, privileged foreign woman, for a bestial slur made by one of my kind and race, a privileged white foreign man, about a dark-skinned woman of Nacho's own race and kind. I could have found out in advance that none of Elvis's acting scenes had been filmed on location and that he was out of favor because of an alleged insult, but I hadn't bothered, assuming a blanket, rosy-hued remembrance of the Hollywood days.

So my vision as press of the divers' world was wrong. Elvis was a persona non grata. Stardom and wealth do not make everyone welcome, and not everyone is happy to smile at the memory of the cameras. My approach was off mark, and what did that say about me? I had thought that I was a friendly person, asking the divers for their memories in the most sincere admiration. But I had believed that what had made the cliff divers famous to "us"—we movie and media consumers of the developed world—was therefore what must make them the most proud, what they must value the most. As performers, they exist for "us," the foreign tourists and image guzzlers. As though our recognition is what "makes" them, and has conceded their fame.

Among Mexicans, Acapulco is also associated with the movies (but primarily with Mexican productions) and immortalized by singers (but Mexican ones, not Elvis Presley). Mexico, a vibrant country of more than one hundred million, has its own lexicon of stardom, silver screen, and discography, different from ours, which is part of its "otherness." I had been barking up the wrong tree. The divers had no end of movies and music with which they were proud to be associated, such as those movies starring María Félix or Tin Tan. Watching Presley's *Fun in Acapulco* recently, I could see why Mexicans would be unimpressed with its crude stereotypes of Mexican characters, exaggerated Mexican accents, and glaring product placement. Moreover, it has the silliest ending, with Elvis singing, of all things, "Guadalajara"—a song devoted to the wrong city in the wrong state. I had started off assuming that the myth was homogenous, that everyone—gringos, Europeans, and Mexicans—had the same stars and common currency of famous people. Not so.

Another thing that was wrong, from the cliff divers' point of view, was my feminist interest in female divers such as Iris, or in Jacqueline Petit. As exceptions to the rule, they did not represent the diver community, but I spent a disproportionate amount of my time pursuing them for interviews and information. It took me a long while to appreciate the divers' reticence with regard to female protagonists and reluctance to allow women on their cliff. Their first reason was the somewhat sexist one that if women did it, it would seem easy! Another one was the distraction of a scantily clad woman on the top of the cliff—the audience may even prefer the women over the men—better eye candy!

**

I had been away from the cliff divers for a long time when I was kindly asked
to contribute this essay. I left Mexico in 2009 after a difficult separation from
my husband in 2007. Such a long time had passed since I had been able to work
on my book project that I feared the divers would forget me or let someone else
write their book. This was very sad for me, the separation—my inability to return
because I could no longer afford the ticket. I last saw them at the end of 2007,
and it was now 2011. My feelings and thoughts were becoming more abstract,
influenced by sensing myself to be a foreigner in my own supposed "home"
(Kent, in South East England). Mexico, where I had lived for fourteen years, and
my beloved Acapulco, were fast becoming a lost home, a land of wasted dreams,
a mysterious paradise that I feared never going to, or immersing myself in, again.

My reading influenced this state of mind and was influenced by it. First was
Jean Rhys's (1982) *Wide Sargasso Sea*, about an abusive marriage between a Cre-
ole girl (Antoinette/"Bertha") and an English colonialist ("Rochester"). I was
somewhat ashamed not to have read this book before, ashamed because I'd been
given to believe that it was something of a feminist and also postcolonial classic,
relevant to my politics and interests as a writer and researcher and to my lived
experience. I'd felt lazy and left behind not being versed in its problematic. And
then, reading about how Rhys had died in relative obscurity, drinking alone, in
Devon or somewhere also remote and in the United Kingdom—the parallels I
could have extrapolated were disquieting.

But what a wonderful book! So vivid, so sad. So torn and emotional and
angry. What an arresting image and symbol, the parrot in flames. And the
vengeance at the end. She knew what she had to do, burn the house down—I
mean the protagonist/heroine, and therefore, the author too. I didn't know what
to do with the story I was trying to write at all.

In April 2011, I signed a contract to complete my book on the Acapulco cliff
divers with Trilce Ediciones in Mexico City. I was happy and relieved about
this, but I was also concerned that after so much time away—from Acapulco
and from my writing—I no longer knew my own voice as a writer (that is, the
voice that was confident and playful, the one that I used to have, and the one
that I wanted to use to write my book). I was too full of longing for a distant
place and its people. Grief at that loss had paralyzed me and left me on the road
to nowhere, with writer's block. Rhys's book chimed with me: having to leave
the "magic" of the exotic, or foreign, world behind. Also in *Wide Sargasso Sea*,

Antoinette joins the ranks of "those who know the secret and will not tell it." I felt I was losing the secret of otherness, of the magic of Acapulco and Mexico, and also losing the power to be able to articulate that secret, and communicate it to my readers. The proximity of violence and cruelty to aching beauty reminded me of Acapulco, even more so since the drug war there had escalated in the years of my absence.[4]

Rhys's book also brought me to my concern as a writer with heightened senses, which I felt affected me in the tropics—partly disorientating, partly enchanting—and with intense emotion, which I felt at the daily death-defying actions of the cliff divers. How to write about these in such a way that my readers would feel at least a frisson, a shiver of strangeness, a thrill of magic, or the beguiling unknown? Was I up to the kind of poetic or melodramatic writing that would be required? The first night of my return to Acapulco in August 2012, I couldn't sleep. When daylight gave me an excuse to wander, wincing at the heat and the glare, I could only bear to look at the tiny things at first: the insects and crabs, then the bird gasping in surprise when I came out onto my balcony at the Hotel Mirador, before he disappeared in a wing-flash of yellow and gray. The sunbathing iguanas below, zigzagging in prehistoric nonchalance between the foliage-spattered rocks.

That kind of intensity and that kind of concertinaed focus of the senses were often equated with illness or insanity. I knew that difference and otherness could easily be written off as madness when they eluded the definitions and rationales of a dominant discourse. Or they could be exoticized as "magic," as in the case of the magical realism genre associated with Latin American writing. I needed confidence in "the secret" that Rhys intimated (as I understood this secret, which was that "magic" is *real*, and "madness" is maligned otherness, inflicted by an inability, or unwillingness, to empathize and understand, or accept its difference),[5] confidence that the luminous, Technicolor world of jagged high cliffs and brave diving men that I had fallen into (after knocking repeatedly at the door)— like Alice into a Wonderland—was not just a figment of my imagination.

Rhys helped me by reminding me that my experience of the magic and the otherness was real, and not just imagined, or madness. I did not have access to anthropological writers such as Frohlich or Harrison (*Being a Tourist*, 2003), who might have helped me theorize and understand my block, or even help me move beyond it. So I returned to other (female) authors who also wrote about place and alienation. Maybe, among their voices, I would find a new voice for myself so that I could resume telling the story. Maybe, with their help, I could construct an appropriate subjectivity, flexible and also strong enough to let "the story" reveal itself.

Kathy Goes to Haiti by Kathy Acker (1990), a book I had read once before, drew me back through its raw and unorthodox confrontation with the subjectivity of a lone American (i.e., First World or privileged—like me) woman finding her way amid much confusion, among local (i.e., "developing world" or less/differently privileged) men in Haiti, an island burdened, like Acapulco, with inequality and corruption. My first thought was that it drew me back because it was female authored and *daring*, and I needed to be daring to write about the cliff divers. Or maybe it was because *they* were daring, and I wanted to live up to them? Or because I had been daring in interviewing and planning a book about them, and, back in England, I no longer felt daring, or able to rise to the challenges I had previously set myself . . .

My questions to Acker were about finding once more my voice as a writer—as with Rhys—but also about anthropological questions into the construction of internal and external (i.e., public) narratives. I thought that she showed the way these jar in her use of the cut-up method of writing, pioneered by William S. Burroughs, and would thus teach me to destabilize the (fallacy of) authorial omniscience and control. The intrepid, shocking, and politically incorrect (or radical) "Kathy" narrates, often deadpan, the adventures of a "Kathy" who is constantly in surreal, and often entertaining, communication with unknown/ unknowable "Natives." While Rhys created a furious lament ending in madness and violence, Acker had created a voice that could encompass displacement and fragmentation, and that was even funny.

My sense of being either fragmented or dispersed, almost painfully intense, once "back there" could seem like "madness." But my fragmentation, my lack of confidence, and the intensity of memories—my "madness"—were also an effect of displacement, the sense of losing self and "home." As I spoke with more and more cliff divers, I found that a number, usually the most risk-loving, were orphaned as children and displaced from the family village or homestead. The inability to feel "at home," even in one's own skin, could become disturbing. Were the divers—who made their symbolic ascent and then plunged into the depths of the Canal de La Quebrada (the Channel of the Gap/Gorge) to emerge, victorious, to loud applause—transcending and conquering these early violations and privations, acting out survival and control in a near impossible situation of danger and threat?

Reading *Kathy* this second time around, I was alternately thrilled and horrified by the way that Kathy, both narrator-protagonist and foreigner-tourist, interacts with local men. (Men are the main economic actors in a culture in which they are the doers and local women tend to stay backstage.) She lets them take advantage of her; she takes advantage of them. Acker finds a variety of ways to write about things that most nonfiction writers find much too embarrassing or difficult. These topics include the reasons that foreigners are tolerated (sex and tourism), the relentless banality of power relations between poorer host and richer guest, and shame. Acker's writing reverberated for me on a personal level too. I owned books of hers, such as *Blood and Guts in High School* (1984), that were too pornographic to leave lying around once I became a mum, and so she became associated with shame (and this was relevant to some of the goings on in Acapulco that I knew about but couldn't write publicly about).

I realize that Rhys also appealed to me for her experimental writing. Rhys—a little like a homeless cuckoo—wrote her story in someone else's nest (taking Charlotte Brontë's 1847 *Jane Eyre* and spelling out, with a new narrative whose protagonist is the violent and ugly "madwoman in the attic," the alienating colonial underbelly of a great British novel). I felt a bit like that, an infiltrator into the cliff divers' world, writing my story inside their stories. I had tried to draw out (or expropriate) the story of Iris Alvarez, the cliff-diving, eleven-year-old girl, hovering about her family nest, to publicize a new story—about women on the cliff—that had not yet been told.

Acker is violent and shocks the reader, and as I returned to my notes and found some of the angry and terrible things that I'd written, I remembered that I'd wanted to do this too. For my reader to take note:

> This is not just a nice story about cliff divers and their historic tradition. . . . Behind the scenes it is about life amid wave after wave of *maltrato (mistreatment, a semi-euphemistic word that the divers used to avoid politics)*, an unequal and brutal society, childhoods torn apart, women discarded, the poor seen as dispensable. It is about the dichotomies of natural beauty and violent human death. It is about spellbinding danger and all the collateral damage that can come of it. Terror and wonder. About courage, the expansion of life, love, strength, and fiction. And about transcendence, death, and letting go.

. . . Too much.

And, on top of all that, what would Jamaica Kincaid say about my ruminations?[6] Was I an ugly, safe, white person, flirting with and aestheticizing the compulsion of these Third World, dark-skinned, vulnerable people who put their lives at risk multiple times per day, for pennies and applause?

Quite possibly. And in the analysis of this problem, I found many valid routes to take:

I could focus on the "uneven exchanges" between myself and the cliff divers that resulted from the "construction and exercise of privilege." How was it that I came to think of them and their story as "mine" to tell (just) because they let me interview them and later send a photographer?

For the construction of my privilege was ample and evident. I was the one who in 2004 had decided that the cliff divers' voices would be interesting to hear and write about. They did not invite me. I used my weight as a journalist accredited by Presidencia (the national government's press office) in my inquiries in Acapulco, where I approached the State Tourism Ministry to request its assistance in finding "Clavadistas de La Quebrada" (divers from La Quebrada Gorge) whom I could speak to for an international project. Thus I came recommended to their association, and their individuals and community, through political and economic authorities, both local and national. My initial writing project, for *Holiday in Mexico*, would be pretty much inaccessible to them—published in a language they didn't read, in a country not their own, and in no way of benefit to them.

Our first interviews fascinated me and revealed to me what I considered to be partly a "gap in the market." These people had great stories to tell, and no one had written a book about them. I was stimulated by the way that some of the divers with whom I spoke were initially wary of me, and I enjoyed the process, as well as the results, of gaining their trust. These were moments when, it seemed to me, hostility turned to hospitality, the chasm of otherness was briefly overcome, and a bridge was (temporarily) forged between our two different worlds.

To cover my transport costs to Acapulco and my time, I decided to write newspaper and magazine articles about different aspects of the cliff divers' history, show, and lifestyles. Doing so had, for me, the advantage of gauging interest on the part of readers and publishers, and of determining whether a book was justified. Also, of showing the cliff divers that I could bring them publicity, persuading them to let me come even closer. I did not ask them what kind of publicity they might like, or whether they wanted a foreign woman like me to be the first person to chart their unique history in a book, or whether they thought that it was a fair exchange that I should benefit from the stories they were kindly telling me, to build a name for myself.

Early on I made a friend who was an anthropologist teaching at UC Berkeley, who recommended that I look at Marcel Mauss's *The Gift* (1966). Later, the notion that the act of giving imposes an obligation helped explain some of the tangles that I encountered during my first eighteen months of research. Indeed, as I worked with more prestigious publications (such as the *Times* of London and the *Wall Street Journal*) and became involved with other influential media (such Radio Mil in the populous Mexico City, Discovery Channel, and TV Globo, one of the biggest television networks in the world), I thought that I was "giving" free publicity to the divers, media coverage, and an improvement in their foreign and local status. It was only later that I realized that some of them were worried that *I* was exploiting *them*. My clumsy (politically), or deft (in media terms), singling out of certain young talents became, initially, a thorn in their side. There I was, splitting allegiances in a tightly knit community—the divers, a lower-class group of racially disparaged "provincial" Mexicans—in whose unity resided their strength to resist manipulation by local politicians and outside interests and to maintain, or improve, their economic well-being.

When I moved back to England, I lost the essential privilege of immersion in the cliff-diver community. Removed from the comfort of the divers' regular friendly comments and reassurance, I started to impose theoretical criticisms on my endeavors to write "their" story, and I gave myself a very hard time. Who did I think I was, with this imperialist urge to consider them "mine," simply because I was the first published, international writer to be taken into their confidence, constructing—with the academic and journalistic privilege I enjoyed—my own "expertise" on Acapulco and "them"?

Meanwhile, the diver community had absorbed my media incursions, my little colonialist invasions, and they had turned everything to their cheerful advantage. In 2007, I had irritated some of the elders by helping enlist a Canadian high dive performing expert to train the younger divers in more varied and safer dives. "We are not circus performers," one said, voice dripping with scorn, and deliberately within my hearing. I hadn't realized that this invitation might ruffle the feathers of macho pride in their sportsmanship. But when I went back for the first time in 2012, those younger divers were the top dogs of the show, their beautiful and breathtaking dives dominating the cliff, and they spoke of what they had learned from Yves Milord with great enthusiasm and even reverence. When I returned in 2013, the diver president for the first time acknowledged the foreigner Jaqueline Petite to have been the first woman to dive in La Quebrada. And when I went back for a third time, during the celebrations of the divers' eightieth anniversary in November 2014, I was embraced warmly by a score of divers as a long lost—although definitely "weird"—auntie-type figure, and I was repeatedly championed for my success in bringing back the "Records Guinness." The cliff divers had forgotten my role in bringing Yves (one of the main things I did for them, or "gave" them), but they welcomed me as "theirs," as family, passing me new babies to fuss over.

Did this interaction suggest a female role that was more comfortable for them rather than one that would involve me in the real male politics of sport and advancement? Or was it a tacit acknowledgement of me as someone who cared for the new generations and had shown my commitment by daring to engage and, though sometimes getting it wrong, persisting over a period of ten years?

I don't know . . . There was no way to control or keep tabs on what they—as a group or individually—thought of me, apart from the fact that they treated me warmly. And as I reflect on that, I suddenly remember their nickname for me! All cliff divers, throughout the generations since 1934, have nicknames that they give to each other, usually in fond mockery, and they stick. In 2006, I brought a photographer—male and Mexican—to portray them for my book, and they gave him a nickname too. I felt a little left out then, but the following year when Yves Milord was training the young divers, I found out that my nickname was "Olivia," after Olive Oyl. This was because Yves—who was very muscular and wore spinach-green swimming trunks with a leaf print—was nicknamed "Popeye," and many of the youngsters had thought that Yves and I were a couple. (That I was "his," maybe?) It was poignant to reflect that I was given my nickname, which meant my acceptance into the language of their world, in relation to a man. I could see that I made more sense that way, rather than as some loose cannon, shifting signifier, double outsider (foreign and female), who belonged apparently to no one (not even one fixed publication) and who turned up when she wanted and wrote (it would have seemed) as she chose. My otherness as a woman in a man's world added new layers and repercussions to the dynamics of privilege and exchange.

Being so removed from La Quebrada and from these dynamics from 2008 to 2012, and taking myself to task so harshly, further dismantled my voice as a writer. I now recognize my writer's voice to be also my voice when I talk to the cliff divers (that voice was partly broken by the long time that I was removed from my diver interlocutors, who engaged with me, challenged me, and allowed me to hear myself as well as them). I was left with a gap or break in the story—the story, I now dare to say, that they and I were creating, together, of La Quebrada.

So—after having gone back to Acapulco and reconnected with the divers, and from then being regularly in touch with the youngsters through Facebook—I started writing again. It is still a challenge to convey the multivocality of this project, but the divers themselves are encouraging me. The hardest part is coming to a conclusion, given that there is no natural end, for the divers continue their labors every day. But now they have become part of my life, through Facebook and WhatsApp, so I no longer have to endure that sense of loss.

Notes

1. These foreign mothers were very similar to women interviewed by Susan Frohlich (2015).
2. This documentary, *Cliff Divers*, was shot, directed, and produced by Simon Stock (2007) in La Quebrada, Acapulco, Mexico. See https://www.doand.co/cliff-divers.
3. I had caused offense, as Behar (2013, 38, 39) did with her uncle in Miami in *Traveling Heavy*.
4. The drug war started in roughly 2004 but escalated in 2006 and has scarred the town to this day (the end of 2018).
5. See Gayatri C. Spivak (2003) on accommodating the undecidable.
6. "The thing you have always suspected about yourself the minute you become a tourist is true: A tourist is an ugly human being. . . . But one day when you are sitting somewhere, alone in that crowd, and that awful feeling of displacedness comes over you . . . you make a leap . . . to being a person visiting heaps of death and ruin and feeling alive and inspired at the sight of it . . . to being a person marvelling at the harmony (ordinarily, what you would say is the backwardness) and the union these other people . . . have with nature" (Kincaid 1988, 14, 16).

References

Acker, Kathy. 1984. *Blood and Guts in High School*. New York: Grove Press.

Acker, Kathy. 1990. *Kathy Goes to Haiti*. London: Flamingo.

Behar, Ruth. 2013. *Traveling Heavy: A Memoir in Between Journeys*. Durham, N.C.: Duke University Press.

Brontë, Charlotte. 1847. *Jane Eyre*. Cornhill: Smith.

Frohlich, Susan. 2015. "'Souvenir Babies' and Abandoned Homes: Tracking the Reproductive Forces of Tourism." *Anthropologica* 57 (1): 63–76.

Guinness World Records. 2007. *Guinness World Records 2008*. New York: Bantam Books.

Harrison, Julia. 2003. *Being a Tourist: Finding Meaning in Pleasure Travel*. Vancouver: University of British Columbia Press.

Kincaid, Jamaica. 1988. *A Small Place*. New York: Farrar, Straus and Giroux.

Mauss, Marcel. 1966. *The Gift: Forms and Functions of Exchange in Archaic Societies*. London: Cohen and West.

Rhys, Jean. 1982. *Wide Sargasso Sea*. London: Norton.

Spivak, Gayatri C. 2003. *Death of a Discipline*. New York: Columbia University Press.

Stock, Simon. 2007. *Cliff Divers*. Discovery Shorts. Filmed in La Quebrada, Acapulco, Mexico.

Wood, Andrew Grant, and Dina Berger, eds. 2009. *Holiday in Mexico: Critical Reflections on Tourism and Tourist Encounters*. Durham, N.C.: Duke University Press.

PART II

Returns

FOUR

Chronicle of a Return to Cuba in a Time of Cholera

RUTH BEHAR

January 8, 2013: On the Way to Cuba, No Longer Sure Whether I Really Want to Go

I've shed my winter coat, and I'm on my way to Cuba. Not alone, but with thirteen undergraduates from the University of Michigan. We meet at the airport in Toronto, though we could fly from Miami with a charter company, but we're closer to the north than the south, and Air Canada is lax about baggage limits, unlike the charter companies in Miami that make a fortune charging for every single ounce over forty-four pounds, including carry-ons. A few students are escorted to the airport by their parents. "You're sure she'll be okay in Cuba?" a mother asks, wrinkling her brow. I reassure her that her daughter will be fine. "Cuba is extremely safe," I respond. I don't tell her that I'm always scared when I go, and yet I keep returning, and now with students to boot. The students are between twenty and twenty-three years old. They're young, very young. Some have never traveled outside the United States. Some have never even left Michigan.

It is my third time taking students to Cuba. I first went in 2010, then again in 2011. For many years I've taught a course called "Cuba and Its Diaspora," and it seemed only natural that I should take students to see the country firsthand so they can witness the complexities of life in Cuba and connect what they've learned from books with the real place. I created our semester abroad program from scratch, and I've worked hard, insanely hard, to maintain it. I believe that it is one of the best contributions I've made as an educator.

An additional motivation behind all that dedication was my desire to spend long periods of time in Cuba. After traveling to Cuba for twenty years on one-week or two-week visits, searching for the lost home of my childhood, I thought that leading the semester abroad program would allow me to lay claim to a life there, not simply be a fleeting visitor from the diaspora who washes in and out of the island like the tides. I receive my regular faculty salary while in Cuba, as though I were teaching in Michigan, but with the added bonus of escaping brutally cold Michigan winters.

Flying to Cuba I always feel uneasy. Despite the numerous return trips, there's that tinge of my parents' ancient fear and paranoia lodged like a bullet in my memory. But this time I feel more uneasy than usual. I carry a secret. A few weeks earlier, while I was packing everything I'd need for my three-month stay in Cuba, a reporter from the *New York Times* called to ask me about my friend Richard Blanco. Richard and I have been friends for about as long as I've been going back and forth to Cuba. The reporter informs me Richard has been chosen by Obama to be the inaugural poet. The news won't be made public until January 8, the day of my departure for Cuba. Don't tell anyone, the reporter says. Don't even call Richard to congratulate him.

As the students sitting near me on the plane doze off listening to music on their iPhones, I think how incredible it is that Richard is about to become a celebrity. I am thrilled for him and want the world to know that he wrote a poem for me, "The Island Within," before he ever knew he'd become famous (Blanco 2012). Soon, though, my mood shifts to self-deprecating. I tell myself that I'm squandering my time taking undergraduates to Cuba. Aren't there more important things I should be doing?

I ponder the political significance of a Cuban American gay poet being cho-sen to represent the United States at a Democratic inauguration (of a president often accused of having communist leanings). That Cubans are not all hard-line exiles seems to be one of the underlying messages. I recall the heartfelt motto of the Cuban Americans of my generation who came to be known as the *maceítos*, the ones who returned to the island, starting in the late 1970s with the Antonio Maceo Brigade: *No todos los cubanos son gusanos* (Not all Cubans are worms). Cubans who chose to leave after Fidel Castro came to power were the "worms of the revolution," and nothing embarrassed my generation more than the idea that we, like our parents who'd taken us away from the island, might be viewed as subhuman because we were no longer living in Cuba. Yet what irony: it was our parents' nostalgia for Cuba that made the island such an intense object of desire. If not for their nostalgia, we wouldn't have cared. Now it dawns on me that I've been acting like the exiles. I've been looking backward for too long, to the place I've lost, not giving attention to the place I've gained, the America in which I live, the country in which I married, had a child, hold a job.

A Cuban woman whom I met in Miami showed me around her federally subsidized apartment. She opened a hall closet and said, "This is where I keep the things to send to Cuba. That's how I live, always thinking about what they need in Cuba." The closet was crammed with clothes, shoes, toys, aspirin, appliances, and a doll with unblinking eyes that stared back at me; the woman's daughter had brought the doll with her into exile.

Have I been living like this woman, advocating for "bridges to Cuba" for so many years? I fantasize that I'll fly to D.C. for the inauguration. Then I'll fly back to Cuba the next day. After all, I have the two passports, the U.S. and the Cuban. I can come and go. I'll hug Richard. I'll acknowledge: yes, I am an American. I used to think that the United States was my nation (the home of my pocketbook) and Cuba my country (the home of my heart). But I'm now feeling that the United States also tugs at my heart, more than I've wanted to realize. I'm proud of Richard and his beautiful poems written in English, our adopted tongue, Shakespeare's tongue.

Still, I stay put in Cuba. On January 21, the day of the inauguration, I rush my students out of class to the apartment where I'm staying, which has access to CNN (there is no reporting in Cuba about Richard being the inaugural poet). We watch Richard read his poem, "One Today," on the television screen.

> . . . hands
> as worn as my father's cutting sugarcane
> so my brother and I could have books and shoes
> (Blanco 2013, 89)

Alluding to sugarcane, Richard references his family's Cuban past. When he finishes, my eyes fill with tears. I cheer, "yay, Richard!" and clap my hands.

The students look at me indifferently. Only one is of Cuban background, from Miami; he had to convince his grandmother of the worthiness of the trip, but he's dryly unsentimental. The others are all *americanos*. They are split evenly between white and African American, and they have gone to Cuba looking for the revolution. Several will purchase Che T-shirts, something I could never do, out of respect for my parents. All of them will express their disgust for tourism in Cuba, feeling shocked about their own privilege and refusing to recognize it. The Cuban American success story bores them. I am part of that story, their professor who rose through the ranks of the academic meritocracy on the back of Mami and Papi's immigrant labor and can now bring students to the country where she no longer lives and get paid for it. The students want the island, the island in its pure form. I can tell already that no matter how much I'll sweat for the next three months to please them, writing comments on their papers, losing sleep to make sure that the program goes smoothly, they're never going to love me. They've come to Cuba in search of a Cuba I can't give them.

January 14, 2013: Saying Good-Bye in Order to Return

In her New Year's Day blog, Yoani Sánchez, the famed Cuban blogger of *Generación Y*, writes, "Someone has to be at the foot of the aircraft steps to say good-bye, holding the handkerchief and wiping their eyes. Someone has to receive the letters, the brightly colored postcards, the long distance phone calls. Someone has to stay and look after the house that was once full of children and relatives. . . . Someone has to stay" (Sánchez 2013). She then lamented, "This 2013, when so many await the implementation of Immigration and Travel Reform, could become a year where we say 'good-bye' many times. While I respect the decision of each person to settle here or there, it doesn't fail to sadden me to see the constant bleeding of creativity and talent suffered by my country." She still ended on a hopeful note, placing herself among those who remain, even though they could leave: "But someone has to stay to close the door, turn the lights off and on again. Many have to stay because this country has to be reborn with fresh ideas, with young people and future proposals."

On January 14, thirteen days later, Yoani Sánchez is among the first to take her place in line when Cuba's new travel and migration law goes into effect. Denied an exit visa twenty times, she was prevented from traveling the world to receive prizes for her blog. After being marooned on the island for twelve years, she receives her passport and sets off on her eighty-day international tour.

I am in Cuba in February when Yoani leaves for her trip. I return to the United States at the end of March just as she's stopping in Miami to meet with all the prominent exile leaders. I wonder why she doesn't meet with those of us who've been trying to build bridges since the late 1970s, the Cuban American professors, writers, and artists who travel back and forth to Cuba with a mix of curiosity, yearning, ambivalence, hope, and fear as we write our books, attend our conferences, and get to know more of the island than our parents ever did. We are not on Yoani's radar. We're not the true representatives of the diaspora, of the "other Cuba," because our stance is too ambiguous. The exiles have stuck to their position; they haven't wavered, even as music from the Buena Vista Social Club thunders in shopping malls in Iowa, even as *National Geographic* features Cuba twice on its cover, even as U.S. religious and medical missions turn the island into a charity hub, even as tourists from around the world grab at every scrap of ruined beauty on the island, even as the remittances of those Cubans who left more recently and have family still in Cuba transform the everydayness of things, quietly but dramatically, one "Just Do It" T-shirt at a time. Among the exiles are my own Mami and Papi, who wait for that future that has yet to arrive. *La espera* that doesn't end. Their position is crystal clear: no Cuba till no Castro . . . now expanded to no Castro in the plural.

I admire the fortitude of the exiles and their ability to conjure Cuba through absence rather than presence. My own position has been that no one can or will take Cuba from me. I seek constant presence, to be there, to stand in the same places I stood as a child, to walk the same streets. Packing and unpacking suit-cases, inhaling and exhaling the air of Cuba, crossing and recrossing geographi-cal borders are the ways that I establish my hold on the island, reclaiming it with my own body and my senses. But since I don't remember Cuba as my parents do, I can't help wondering whether this is an experiment in futility, an effort to salute my absence. I once thought that I'd end up in Cuba one day. Lately I feel that I'm growing too old to imagine a future for myself on the island. The health system is much touted in Cuba, but I pray never to fall ill while I'm there.

After returning to the United States with the students at the end of March, I go back to Cuba in mid-May to spend a week in Havana with a professor-friend in search of Cuban science fiction books that he wants to translate and publish. We end up meeting a *librero*, half-genius, half-madman, who sells books from the patio of his house. He has a room filled from floor to ceiling with books, many of which are censored books not found in Cuban bookstores. He tells us that he has to put things in order and see with whom he'll hide the many dangerous books he carries—*porque la cosa se va a poner dura, ya pronto vuelve la bloguera*. He doesn't dare mention Yoani Sánchez by name, but he says they're going to crack down on all peddlers of ideas once she's back.

As she stated in her blog, someone has to stay. Dissidence in Cuba has been a matter of departure, of immigration, for far too long. Someone has to stay. Someone has to say good-bye in order to return.

February 15–17, 2013: In This Time of Cholera

Havana resident Osvaldo Pino Rodríguez, a forty-six-year-old barber, dies of cholera on January 6, two days before I arrive with the students. But the news of a cholera outbreak isn't reported in the *Granma* newspaper until January 15, and then only as an "Informative Note to the Public." The outbreak begins at the Latin American stadium in El Cerro. The explanation I hear is that it was caused by Tan Rico soda pop kept cold in buckets of dirty ice. The melted drops that dripped into people's mouths from the soda cans caused the contamination. Before that, there was cholera in Holguín in December, and before that, people say it came from Haiti, where seven thousand people have died of cholera since that country's 2010 earthquake. The Cuban Health Ministry reports fifty-one cases and many suffering from "diarrheal diseases." An anticholera campaign sweeps through Havana and the island. Bottles of a diluted bleach solution, as well as a cloth soaked with the solution to clean the bottom of people's shoes, appear at the entrance to schools, public buildings, stores, restaurants, and night clubs. I receive a concerned email from my university. Are we taking all the necessary precautions? I reply that we are.

And then one of my students becomes ill with diarrhea and vomiting. The student, two of her roommates, and I rush to the international health clinic on a Friday night. The student is seen right away. After ascertaining that she has a fever, the doctor sends us by ambulance to the Institute for Tropical Medicine, which is twenty-five miles from Havana. He says that she needs to be tested for cholera. We are at the institute for three hours. After running tests, the doctors determine that my student doesn't have cholera.

It is up to me to figure out how to get us all back to Havana in the dead of night. Fortunately, a young man I know who dreams of leaving for Canada one day responds to my phone call and gives us a ride.

I think I am done dealing with the cholera scare. A few days later another student falls ill at three o'clock in the morning. Her roommate calls asking me to take them to the doctor. I am worn out, I've been sleeping badly, and I know there will be yet another trip to the Institute for Tropical Medicine. I suggest that they either go on their own or wait until morning when one of the program staff can accompany them to the doctor in an official car. The student is taken to the doctor that morning and then to the Institute for Tropical Medicine. No cholera is found. By the next day she is completely recovered.

But the student reveals to me, a week later, that she has been stewing in her fury toward me.

She is a tall, statuesque woman, with long curly hair, as beautiful as a model. I feel myself shrivel as she reprimands me. "You should have been there for me, you should have taken me to the doctor, even if it was three in the morning," she exclaims.

I realize she is right. I realize how lucky we are that things didn't go terribly wrong. We were spared a tragedy. What if she'd been seriously ill? What if she'd died? I am aware, suddenly, of the huge responsibility that I've taken on in choosing to bring American students to Cuba.

My tears start to flow. "I'm sorry," I say. She looks at me pityingly, the professor she once admired.

She forgives me, but I don't forgive myself.

The specter of cholera haunts me for the rest of my stay with the students. Where have I brought them? I ask myself. A country where there is filth in the water, a country where buildings are in ruin and collapse every day, sometimes burying those inside with no mention anywhere of these losses. This native land that I have wanted to reclaim for the last twenty years, this land that had a beautiful utopian dream of health and education triumphing over poverty and injustice, is a place harboring a disease as primitive as the plague.

March 5, 2013: Death of Chávez

A veil of silence falls over Havana following the death of Hugo Chávez. I consider canceling my class so that the students and I can go to the Plaza de la Revolución for the march in honor of Chávez, but I decide that it will be more beneficial for us to discuss in the classroom the meaning of his death for Cubans. One student says that seeing the reaction to Chávez's death is a way to imagine what it will be like when Fidel goes. It's an insightful remark. I think about how terrified I am of being in Cuba when that event finally happens—Fidel's funeral.

Music isn't heard on the pedestrian walkway of Calle Obispo for several days. People express fear that the island might return to the same sorrowful state as in the days of the special period—hunger, austerity, no gasoline, no transportation, and worst of all, *apagones*. Darkness.

But afterward things quickly slip back into a kind of normal. I find myself at a dinner party with a group of successful artists—one lives in Cuba but now spends a large amount of time in Miami; one lives in New York but now spends more time in Cuba; another lives in Germany and comes back every year for several months; one experimented with living in Spain but ultimately came back to Cuba, which is the fountain of inspiration. We talk about the theme of returning, how a distinction no longer exists between *cubanos de afuera* and *cubanos de adentro*, between Cubans who live on the island and Cubans who live outside the island. With almost a quarter of the Cuban population now living abroad as permanent immigrants or as a floating island of migrants, one simply asks, *¿Eres cubano?* "Are you Cuban?" Upon receiving a yes, one asks, *¿De qué ciudad? ¿Cubano de dónde?* "Cuban from what city? Cuban from where?" You can be a Cuban New Yorker, a Cuban Catalan, a Cuban Berliner. Residing elsewhere doesn't make you any less Cuban than being a full-time islander.

Restaurants have sprung up in Havana that are little vessels of hope in a more open economy. With new property laws in place, *cubanos* who migrated and returned with hybrid identities and money in their wallets have bought houses and apartments and transformed them virtually overnight into swanky private enterprises. Mediterraneo Havana serves homemade pasta and its own pecorino and mozzarella cheese, and it is owned by a migrant who lived in Sardinia for eight years and considers himself a *cubano-italiano*. On his return, he brought along an Italian chef and a chef from Barcelona. Porto Habana is the creation of a *cubano-portugués* who lived in Portugal for twelve years. He serves Cuban food on the wraparound balcony of his eleventh-floor apartment, the breezes flowing from the ocean. Matter-of-factly, he announces that he has traveled around the entire world and yet is glad to be home. He saw many beautiful places, but he was always lonely, missing his family and friends, missing Cuba. Business is going well. If he gets bored, he catches a flight to Miami and visits his cousins. I can barely believe what I'm hearing. Echoes of the days when wealthy Cubans would travel to Miami on weekends to go shopping.

And that appears to be the wave of the future. Mobile Cubans with more than one passport, more than one nationality. Our portable island that fits in a suitcase. There were the years of the PRE (Permiso de Residencia en el Exterior), when people could travel and come back within eleven months and not lose their Cuban citizenship. Now with up to two years to be away and not lose your *libreta* (should you wish to keep receiving rationed food at your local *bodega*) nor your house nor your citizenship, many are making their way to the United States, staying a year and a day under the generous laws that make it easy for Cubans to get their green cards. The aim of this latest wave of migrants is not to stay in the United States permanently but to be able to go back and forth. And no one will call them *gusanos* or *escoria*, neither "worms" nor "scum."

I have to admit that I feel jealous of these Cuban puddle jumpers. They won't suffer the humiliation and sorrow of being stripped of their homes and citizenship as was true of exiles like my parents who left in the early years of the revolution. They can return and buy property, which I cannot do. Globalization has softened Cuban nationalist zeal. So too have Cuba's debt and the need for hard currency.

The fierce years of treating immigration as a political act, as a form of transgression, seem to be over on the island. They have given way to the idea that Cubans can and should disperse themselves around the world. Indeed, they should ransack places far and wide, bleed the capitalist nations, and bring the wealth back to the island that still declares itself socialist against all odds. Leave, but triumph. Leave, but bring your money back to the homeland. The new "New Man" is a global Cuban, a world traveler, thoroughly cosmopolitan. The latest political billboards, placed strategically on the way to the José Martí airport, state in no uncertain terms, *Los cambios en Cuba son para Más Socialismo* (The changes in Cuba are for More Socialism).

After decades of immigrants being demonized in Cuban popular perceptions, outward migration has come to be associated with success. Failure is the result of confinement within national borders. Not that Cuba is unique in holding such perceptions. The idea that mobility engenders privilege has become widespread. As Zygmunt Bauman (1998, 121) suggests in his book *Globalization: The Human Consequences*, "Today's existence is stretched along the hierarchy of the global and the local, with global freedom of movement signalling social promotion, advancement and success, and immobility exuding the repugnant odour of defeat, failed life and being left behind."

Those who are immobile will suffer the curse of being unable to move, of being stuck, of staring at the sea, of wondering what lies beyond. They might get a thrill muttering *gusano* under their breath when they wave good-bye to yet another vagabond, but they'll dream of the day when they too can go elsewhere . . . whether for a few years, or forever.

March 24, 2013: Leaving Cuba Again, as I Always Do, the Gift That Mami and Papi, the *Gusanos*, Gave Me

Our semester abroad program ends, and I leave Cuba with the students. Over the course of three months, I've taken the students on trips all over Cuba, to visit Catholic churches, Santería shrines, a Chinese community center, Jewish synagogues in Havana and the provinces, art museums, artist studios, colonial and modern architecture, archaeological sites, nature reserves, provincial cities, and the major neighborhoods of Havana. We've traveled the island from end to end. I've introduced them to brilliant artists and dedicated scholars. I've given numerous hours to the students to discuss their ideas, their thoughts on Cuba. I've taught them how to do research and watched them make progress on their writing. I've opened my apartment to them in the evening when they wanted to watch the Super Bowl or just sit and talk and eat ice cream. I've set up salsa dance classes for those who were interested. I've done everything for them that I would have wanted a teacher to do for me.

I hope for a few kind words on my course evaluations. Fortunately, several students will say that Cuba transformed them and that they're grateful for the experience. But the handful of criticisms will cut scars into my soul. One student will dismiss the trips that we took around the island as nothing more than tourism. Another will write on the evaluation, "We visited too many synagogues."

Cuba is a difficult place to be, *no es fácil*, unless you have family or friends or memories to seek, or you are a photographer or filmmaker. The white students are mistaken for tourists and hassled on the street by hawkers selling everything from towels to car rides. The African American students are mistaken for Black Cubans and asked by the police for identification. The students all share an apartment in a Havana building, and they experience the *apagones* and the elevator that is constantly breaking, requiring they walk up and down fourteen flights of stairs, and though they receive breakfasts and dinners that are hearty by Cuban standards, the meals are not as bountiful as they're used to. I feel for the students and all they've put up with to be in Cuba. It would have been much easier to spend a semester in Spain or Chile, but they chose Cuba.

So I'm truly touched that several are sorry that our program isn't continuing for another three months. They've come to desire Cuba as I do, even with all its flaws. They want to stay and just be in Cuba, without having to take courses, without having to do schoolwork. They want to live like real Cubans. They even resent the 24-7 internet connection that I made sure they had, so they could be on Facebook all the time, something that I thought they couldn't live without.

But they feel that I've kept them from having an authentic experience of Cuba. A few are plotting to return on their own in the summer, if they can scrape up the money.

Arriving on the other side, bringing them all home safely, I honestly want to bend down and kiss the ground, but I just do so mentally. Then I hug each of them good-bye, polite teacher that I am.

I've left Cuba with them, and they know I could have stayed if I'd wanted to. They know that the island waits for me. They know I'll go back again and again.

November 4, 2018: *Después*, Afterward . . .

I have continued to go to Cuba again and again, but I no longer travel with students. In 2014, the newly hired director of travel abroad programs at my university decided to streamline the process of taking students to Cuba. The program was reduced first to six weeks in May–June and then to three weeks in May. Rather than the program being designed by a professor working directly with a Cuban institution, as had been the case during the three times that I took students to Cuba, the organization of the program was handed over to an "academic service provider." The provider is an American-based company, making the financing easier and the managerial work less time consuming for the university. Services can be paid for directly in the United States, and all the responsibilities are handed over to the intermediary. The provider has an administrative staff in Cuba that organizes everything for the students, including trips, lectures, meals, and housing. This system of academic tourism allows faculty without knowledge or background on Cuba, even those who don't speak Spanish, to accompany students and enjoy a trip to the island.

I was saddened by this decision and shed many tears when I received the news. I felt that I'd been a fool, giving up years of my life for a program in Cuba that ended instantly with the stroke of an administrator's pen. Taking American students to Cuba had been a less joyful journey than I had expected when I started out, but there was a part of me that still wanted to keep on going. I pictured myself years into the future, old, gray, stumbling with my suitcases, still taking students to Cuba, dreaming of the day that I would make everything perfect, for the students and for me.

I knew that my trips to Cuba with the students hadn't been a total failure. A few students had gone on to do graduate work in Cuba. A few had returned to Cuba on their own and established connections with communities there. A few had written later to say how much the experience of being in Cuba with me had meant to them, though they couldn't see it at the time. This was consoling, but a door had closed, and I didn't want to travel to Cuba with students on the new program organized by the academic service provider.

Then, in July 2017, something marvelous happened. I co-led a trip with Richard Blanco—the two of us traveling together to Cuba as we'd dreamed—just a year after the reopening of the United States Embassy in Havana, when we were filled with hope for the future of normalized relationships between our two countries. Richard and I took a group of twenty young Cuban Americans to the island, visiting for the first time on a cultural heritage trip with the CubaOne Foundation.[1] I found myself exhilarated being in Cuba with young people who cared about everything that I had to say and share and show them about Cuba. They understood the emotional turmoil of returning to Cuba. They understood the sorrow of loss and the ambivalent desire to claim a place that our parents and grandparents had fled and never been able to forget. I felt their love. So much love.

I realized then that this was what I'd wanted from the students, something so simple, just their love. But they didn't love me, and that broke my heart. Even now, years later, I think back to that trip to Cuba in a time of cholera and wonder what in the world I could have done to win their love, and knowing that the answer is nothing breaks my heart all over again.

Note

1.   For more on the CubaOne Foundation, see the organization's website at: http://cubaone.org/.

References

Bauman, Zygmunt. 1998. *Globalization: The Human Consequences*. New York: Columbia University Press.

Blanco, Richard. 2012. "The Island Within." In *Looking for the Gulf Motel*, 16–17. Pittsburgh, Pa.: University of Pittsburgh Press.

Blanco, Richard. 2013. *For All of Us, One Today: An Inaugural Poet's Journey*. Boston: Beacon Press.

Sánchez, Yoani. 2013. "In 2013: Reasons to Stay." *Generación Y* (blog). January 1, 2013. https://generacionyen.wordpress.com/2013/01/01/in-2013-reasons-to-stay/.

FIVE

Postcards from Cancún

M. BIANET CASTELLANOS

September 2000

As the plane descends, I see beneath me the flatness of the Yucatán Peninsula bordered by pale strips of white sand and the immense turquoise waters of the Caribbean Sea. From up here, the jungle that stretches beyond the horizon is stopped in its tracks by Cancún's concrete existence. Seductively, it offers this city an *abrazo*, an embrace that must be carefully contained and culti-vated by government officials, squatters, and land developers. The mangroves of the Laguna Nichupté separate the bulk of the peninsula from Cancún's Zona Hotelera (hotel zone), a narrow strip of land in the shape of the number seven delicately tethered to the mainland, seemingly capable of floating away by the force of a strong hurricane. Anchored by massive hotels, the Zona Hotelera avoids such a fate. This aerial view makes evident the spatial differences that divide the international tourist strip of Cancún from its commercial center, its outlying shantytowns, and the tropical jungle of the peninsula. Few visitors notice the physical, cultural, linguistic, ethnic, and class barriers that separate these spaces, and even fewer attempt to cross them. Yet these spaces are inter-connected and interdependent; Cancún could not exist without the presence of the rural villages that dot the hinterland of the peninsula and the shantytowns that divide the Zona Hotelera from the jungle. By narrating my experiences traveling between Cancún and the rural Maya village of Kuchmil, half of whose population works in Cancún, I map out the "emotional residue" that results from the imposition of these physical, cultural, linguistic, and economic barriers (Anzaldúa 1987, 3).[1]

When the seatbelt light turns off, I grab my bags and follow the other passengers, the majority of whom are tourists from the Midwest eager to start their vacation. A few passengers are Mexicans returning home after vacationing in the United States or sojourning home as a brief respite from work there. I too am returning "home" to the country of my birth, but as I am an anthropologist who has been working in the Yucatán Peninsula since 1991 and who was raised in California, Cancún is for me a field site rather than a playground. As we follow the signs to Mexican customs, a metal railing prevents us from entering the waiting area. We are shuttled directly from a crowded airplane full of gringos to a long line of foreigners waiting for clearance from immigration.[2] This process is routine and efficient; no one is singled out or harassed, despite the presence of stoic soldiers in green army fatigues. Unlike the northern border checkpoints in Houston (which I traverse on my return to the United States) and Tijuana (which I would visit soon after moving to San Diego in 2001), where the unease is palpable among those waiting in line and where the U.S. border patrol agents flex their power as they fix their gaze on the crowd—made up primarily of Mexicans and Mexican Americans—and attempt to trip our tongues into making verbal mistakes that mark us as "alien," this border checkpoint is tense not with fear but with excitement of the upcoming days of sun, sea, alcohol, and the exotic. "Mexico Welcomes You!" a large sign reminds us.

Although the month of September is considered part of the low tourist season, the airport is teaming with tourists, primarily from the United States. When I walk through the sliding glass doors that separate the duty-free internationally neutral buffer zone of baggage claim, I am now *in* Mexico. Hotel chauffeurs and travel agents form a crowd outside the doors in the airport lobby; they hold up signs listing names of clients and hotel corporations. While the *maleteros* (baggage helpers) run up to offer their services to luggage-laden tourists, the bus drivers yell out the time for the next bus departing for Playa del Carmen, a tourist site located south of Cancún that, within the next decade, will become the most popular tourist destination in the Americas. I walk through the liminal space that this lobby creates, where foreigners can access ATMs, rent cars, make hotel reservations, and purchase something to eat in their native tongues. Spanish is not needed here. As I exit the air-conditioned airport lobby, I am slightly shocked by the heat of the afternoon sun. Eager tour guides surround me, wishing to make my time in Cancún a truly extraordinary experience. In English, German, French, and Italian, they ask, "Do you want to go to Playa del Carmen?" "Do you want to swim with the dolphins?" "Do you want to have a great time?" In this enclosed space, Cancún becomes a spectacle of consumption, peddled shamelessly to capture tourists' attention and their money.

The international airport is located approximately twenty minutes outside the city of Cancún. The elite ride in the courtesy hotel minivan, rent a car, or take a taxi priced between forty and sixty U.S. dollars. Those on a tight budget or with time to spare take the *transporte compartido* (shuttle), referred to locally as a *combi*, for a reduced rate of seven U.S. dollars.[3] Since I have more time than money to spare, I pay my seven dollars to get on the *combi*, whose last stop will be the bus station downtown where I can catch a bus that will take me to the neighboring state of Yucatán. I am told that there is no other way to get to Cancún, but I wonder how the airport workers get to work. Eventually I find out that the state subsidizes a bus line for employees and local residents. For an extra two dollars on top of the six-peso fee (sixty-five cents), a price that is five times less expensive than the *combi* and fifteen times less expensive than a taxi, this bus will also transport tourists downtown. But this time I do not see and am not told about the bus. In 2002, airport renovations forced the bus stop to be moved to a more visible location, right across the parking lot from the international arrival gate.[4]

The *combi*, a Suburban sport utility vehicle painted white and yellow, the colors of the airport transportation system, is air-conditioned and spacious. I sit next to two American women while we wait for a couple of newlyweds and a businessman to get on board. Once we get on our way, the show literally begins. The television in the *combi* displays an English-speaking host who guides us through the wonders of Cancún: dancing, eating, playing, and sunbathing. I skip the show to watch the scenery; I am anxious to glimpse the ocean again before I depart Cancún. Surface water is rare in the southeastern section of the peninsula where I am headed because the porous limestone terrain quickly absorbs rainwater. As we exit the airport, large billboards advertise the attractions of Cancún, its shopping centers, ecological parks, hotels, and restaurants, all of which are owned by transnational corporations such as American Express, Hilton Hotels, and Tony Roma's. The *combi* speeds down the highway, passing by the occasional business and the elite Universidad La Salle, a preparatory school and university. We admire the raw beauty of the landscape; the dense jungle and the lack of buildings, houses, and strip malls along the highway cater to tourists' desire for the exotic. Hidden behind this wall of foliage, however, are multinational hotels, small fishing villages, housing developments, squatter settlements, and ecological parks, all of which compromise if not destroy the ecosystem that tourists admire so much. The sealed *combi* prevents us from smelling the stench of the city's infamous *aguas negras* (sewage water), a foul smell that serves as the local metaphor for the destruction of this ecosystem.

To access the hotels in the Zona Hotelera, tourists need not traverse the crowded streets of Cancún's commercial center. After fifteen minutes, highway signs inform us that Cancún Centro is straight ahead, but the driver veers right for the Zona Hotelera and soon presents us with a stunning view of clear ocean waters and white sandy beaches. During the next forty minutes, we drop off passengers at lush resorts built in varied designs from Spanish haciendas (plantations) to Maya pyramids surrounded by landscapes of rolling green lawns, gardens full of bright pink bougainvillea, and tall palm trees that flourish year-round in the heavy tropical heat. The Zona Hotelera is kept immaculate and well manicured through a cooperative effort by the city, federal government, and multinational hotels. Islands of open-air markets and air-conditioned shopping malls break up the monotony of the hotel strip. The shops sell gold and silver jewelry, beautiful crafts from distinct regions of Mexico, and clothes from international designers, such as Massimo, DKNY, GUESS, and Zara. In the Zona Hotelera, travelers encounter what they seek: a tamed and contained lush tropical paradise.

As we enter Cancún's *centro*, or commercial center, the vastness and spaciousness of the Zona Hotelera disappears. The international success of Cancún attracted a large influx of migrants, converting Cancún into the fastest-growing city in the country. Land has become scarce, while population growth, inflation, and avarice increase housing costs. The *centro* grew simultaneously with Cancún's development; this area is provided with amenities available in most cities, including garbage collection, piped water, paved roads, public transportation, hospitals, schools, and parks. Businesses cater to tourists looking for cheaper prices and seeking a more multicultural experience than what is offered in the Zona Hotelera. Businesses also cater to the needs of the middle class who live here and the working class who shop here. All bus routes end and begin here. Such activity generates a constant flow of traffic, both automotive and human, that congests the streets and sidewalks.

The commercial center serves as a buffer zone between the Zona Hotelera and the surrounding shantytowns (also known as *regiones, colonias,* or working-class neighborhoods), which offer shelter to the thousands of service workers who provide cheap labor for the tourist industry and for the nouveau riche, the latter of whom acquired their wealth by supplying services and goods to the working class. Service workers are taught to engage tourists in conversations and to cultivate friendships. Yet few tourists see the neighborhoods in which the employees of the tourist industry live. In the *regiones,* as these neighborhoods are called by local residents, few trees dot the landscape, parks consist of concrete playgrounds and sandy soccer fields, trash settles everywhere, and unpaved, unmarked streets divide up the blocks of housing under construction. These concrete neighborhoods replace the protective shade of the lush lowland tropical jungle with dusty roads and intense heat. As funds trickle in, the city will incorporate these neighborhoods by paving roads and building schools and parks. In the meantime, residents find it difficult to preserve the jungle foliage while constructing their homes on the 160 square meters allocated to them by the state. Renters live in tiny cramped rooms with one small window for ventilation. During the dry winter months, the strong winds blow trash into neighbors' yards and coat the furniture and floors with fine layers of dust. The heat, the dust, and the dry brush create a desert-like environment on the edge of a tropical forest. Aided by the lack of a drainage system, the heavy summer rains transform the unpaved streets into rivers that sweep away the scattered trash. Although ecologically degraded, the *regiones* provide affordable housing for Cancún's booming migrant population, especially for Maya migrants from the state of Yucatán.

But I cannot see the *regiones* from the *centro's* busy streets. The *combi* driver drops me off at the bus terminal located on Tulum Avenue, the *centro's* main thoroughfare. Originally a single, small building that housed both first- and second-class buses, this building was renovated and expanded in the year 2000, resulting in a spatial reorganization according to ticket price (e.g., premier and first- and second-class buses) and hence by social class. I purchase a first-class ticket to Valladolid because first class guarantees me access to an air-conditioned bus, a seat, a movie (usually an action flick), a bathroom, and most importantly, the right to travel on the *autopista,* or toll road, which shaves two hours off of my otherwise four-hour trip. The second-class bus is much cheaper because it travels along a public-access highway, requiring it to make stops in each village that it passes, and it lacks air-conditioning or a bathroom. The absence of these amenities makes for an excruciatingly slow, hot, and uncomfortable trip, particularly if one is traveling with a family or doesn't get a seat and must stand for the whole journey. Most migrants prefer to travel on the first-class bus or take a *combi* to Valladolid, especially if they are traveling with children.

The afternoon bus heading for Merida with a stop in Valladolid is full of student travelers, businessmen and women, and migrants making a trip home. This time I am seated next to a young gentleman who pulls out a newspaper to read on the trip. As I settle into my assigned seat, I salute my neighbor, as is customary in Mexico. Since the air-conditioning system works too well on these buses, I put on a fleece sweater that I packed for this occasion. After a long day of traveling, I am too tired to converse or watch the movie. I promptly fall asleep to the rhythm of the stops and starts required by Cancún's busy streets. On the open highway, there is little to see from the *autopista* beyond dense jungle. The toll road cuts a straight line from city to city, avoiding the twists, turns, and *topes* (speed bumps) of the public highway that connects villages and towns across the peninsula.

I am awakened by the bus driver's announcement that we have arrived on the outskirts of Valladolid. Passengers for whom this is their final destination are told to unload their luggage. Another bus will take us to the city's *centro*. The remaining passengers are given a fifteen-minute break to purchase food and souvenirs at the rest stop's gift shops and restaurants. The smokers among us stand by the bus puffing on their cigarettes. Those of us traveling to Valladolid, mainly women and children, gather at the end of this mini-mall to wait for our bus. While most people may not know each other, we have a destination in common, a city with a small-town feel and sense of decorum; we greet each other, chat about the weather, and help each other load our suitcases onto the old bus waiting to take us into town.

As the bus rumbles south, we share the road with dark-skinned Maya men dressed in stained work shirts, Panama hats, tattered trousers, and thick leather *huaraches* (sandals) who amble by on horseback or bicycles after a long day of working in their *milpas* (cornfields). Mestizas, freshly bathed and wearing baby-blue *huipiles* decorated with brightly colored, embroidered floral designs on the sleeves and hems, dresses that mark them as Indigenous women from the towns neighboring Valladolid, also cruise by on their bicycles. Although the sun is going down, the heat hovers in the air. The wide highway eventually narrows into a cobblestoned street. The bus squeezes through the corridor of Spanish colonial homes built on high sidewalks and recessed a couple of feet from the street. The dark wooden double doors typical of this architectural style open directly onto the street, giving us a clear view of the interior parquet floors, cool whitewashed stone walls, and high ceilings marked by dark wood beams. The residents of these homes, many of whom are descendants of the Spanish elite who replaced the ancient Maya ceremonial center of Zací with the city of Valladolid, sit in chairs of sturdy wood or wrought iron, placed near the entryway to their homes. They fan themselves with Chinese paper fans and murmur *buenas tardes* (good evening) to the people passing by.

We turn the corner at the main plaza, whose center consists of a garden park where lovers take their evening stroll and families purchase *paletas* (ice cream) and *palomitas* (popcorn) for their children after attending mass in the majestic stone cathedral of San Gervasio. A statue, not of a Spanish conquistador or an ex-president but of a fair-skinned mestiza dressed in a *huipil* and carrying a water jug, stands in the center of this park. The mestiza serves as the central motif of the city because Valladolid, or Zací as it continues to be called, has remained the commercial epicenter for the Maya villages of the southeastern peninsula for the past five centuries. *Combis* and buses full of Maya campesinos (day laborers), *muchachas* (maids), maquiladora (factory) workers, vendors, artisans, and students flood the city daily. Maya is shouted here, not murmured like in Cancún. The work and social pace of life is slower in Zací due to the intense heat and the emphasis on a decorum that requires one to greet and converse with a neighbor, customer, and relative.

The buses and *combis* that go to the Maya village of Kuchmil do so only twice a day. Migrants with little time to spare pay the fifteen-dollar taxi fare in order to get to Kuchmil the same day. It is too late to catch the 5:00 p.m. bus to Kuchmil, so I walk a few blocks to the home of friends. Don Enrique May Kauil and doña Olga Can Tun left Kuchmil in 1992 after a political fallout. Kuchmil is organized around an *ejido* system, where land is inalienable and held collectively, and members have the right to work the land. During his tenure as *comisario municipal* (mayor) of Kuchmil in the early 1990s, don Enrique clashed with the political faction led by don Dani Can Balam, who accused him of pocketing government subsidies for his own benefit. The new administration threatened to take away his *ejido* rights.[5] Disillusioned and wishing to avoid further conflict after don Dani took over as *comisario municipal*, don Enrique fled with his family to the home of his wife's brother in Zací. While he retained his rights to his *ejido* land, he didn't have the money to travel back and forth between Kuchmil and Zací. Now he alternates between working as a garment

worker in a maquiladora and as an itinerant *panadero* (bread vendor) cruising
the streets in the early hours of the morning on a bright yellow tricycle. Using a
special whistle whose iconic sound signals the *panadero*'s presence, don Enrique
sells bread out of a large, round, silvery tin basket resting precariously within a
square metal frame fixed to the front of the tricycle. Since working-class families
need multiple incomes to survive, doña Olga alternates between working as a
domestic servant and as a garment worker. Their two eldest daughters also work
in maquiladoras, while their youngest children attend school.

Berenice, Julia, and Lina sit talking to their friends on their front porch as
I walk up to their house. When they recognize me, they wave happily with
faces full of surprise. I couldn't tell them of my plans to visit Yucatán because
they don't have a telephone and mail is sporadically distributed in their barrio
(neighborhood). Lina runs inside to inform her parents that I have arrived,
while Berenice and Julia rush to help me with my bags. Don Enrique and doña
Olga greet me with the great enthusiasm and warmth characteristic of their
personalities. We spend the evening sitting in hammocks that stretch across the
spacious kitchen, the coolest room in the house, updating each other on all that
has occurred since my last visit, the year before. By the time that I depart for
Kuchmil the next day, I will know who died, was born, married, and migrated
from Kuchmil during my absence.

The next morning I board an old creaky bus that appears to be a retired
American school bus painted white with green and brown stripes. People stare
at me as I drag my backpack and grocery bags up the stairs. Families in Kuchmil
cultivate and harvest most of their food. To avoid burdening my host, I always
bring dry food supplies like rice, pasta, and cereal. Before I know it, my load is
lightened by a gentleman who helps push my bags onto the bus and then onto
the overhead luggage rack. "Dios b'óotik," I thank him politely.[6] The passengers
smile widely at my ability to speak Maya. "Tu'ux ka bin?" They ask where I am
heading. "Tin bin Kuchmil," I respond. They nod their heads in recognition
of this place. The children laugh at my accent. This bus's route travels through
the pueblos (small villages) in the southeastern part of the peninsula that have
always been predominantly Maya.[7] The men are dressed in shirts and trousers.
Some of the women wear *huipiles*, while others wear skirts and blouses. They
all speak Maya. Usually I recognize passengers on the bus, but this time I see
no familiar faces.

When the driver enters the bus, his gaze is drawn to mine. Although I am
of average height in the United States, I am tall among Yucatec Maya people,

who constitute one of the shortest populations in the Americas. I feel even taller on this particular bus because the luggage rack hangs low and the knee space is limited. The driver notices my large travel backpack and assumes that I have boarded the wrong bus because only tourists carry such backpacks. In Spanish, he politely informs me, "This bus is heading south toward Carrillo Puerto." The town of Felipe Carrillo Puerto was originally founded by the rebel Maya who fought in the Caste War of 1847–1901. Kuchmil sits along the road heading to this town. "I'm going to Kuchmil," I respond. "Why are *you* going to Kuchmil?" he asks with a suspicious look. I state simply, "I'm an anthropologist and will be working in Kuchmil." "Ahhh," he murmurs and stops asking questions. A young man sitting behind me mentions that he knows quite a few anthropologists who have come to work in his village of Chan Kom, a community well known among anthropologists due to the seminal work of Robert Redfield. "Do you know an *antropóloga* who is an *española*?" He tells me her name, but I don't recognize it. Later when I read Alicia Re Cruz's *The Two Milpas of Chan Kom* (1996), I realize that he was referring to her work. Most everyone I encounter around these parts seems to know an anthropologist by name. For the past century, anthropologists and archaeologists have been frequently drawn to the pyramids and people of this region.[8]

    With a loud throttle, the bus pulls out of the station. The trip will take approximately two hours due to periodic stops at each village along the route and to the speed bumps purposely placed to prevent the accidental deaths of children and animals crossing the road. I converse with the young man until he disembarks at Chan Kom. I spend the rest of the trip trying to notice the changes, if any, that have transformed the landscape since my last visit. With the exception of certain Catholic churches, few colonial buildings exist on the periphery of Zací. Villages are composed of the government *palacio* (palace) and clusters of homes, a mixture of traditional oval-shaped homes made of wood with *palapa* (palm thatch) roofs, a design dating back to pre-Columbian times, and stone homes belonging to more established families. Packs of turkeys and herds of pigs wander across the village *k'íiwiks* (main plazas), while young boys play soccer in this grassy space. I notice that the road runs straight through a pyramid mound near the village of Xanlah. In *Nine Mayan Women* (1976), Mary Elmendorf mentioned that a pre-Hispanic grave was found in this village. A few homes have been converted to Pentecostal churches; a simple wooden cross marks them as temples. With the exception of these new churches, the new coats of paint that each municipal president adds to the public buildings, and the new homes being built by migrants, little appears to have changed. As the bus turns the familiar curve leading into Kuchmil, this façade of tranquility and timelessness hides from view the complex ties and lives connecting Kuchmil to Cancún.

December 2011

"¡Feliz año nuevo!" Periodically, I receive text messages like this one from my friends in Kuchmil and their relatives in Zací and Cancún. I no longer need to travel to stay updated on friends' lives. In 1991, there were two ways to communicate with the residents of Kuchmil. The first was by transportation: by foot, bicycle, car, or bus. The second was by a pay phone whose service was rendered untrustworthy due to faulty wiring. The neighboring town had a public phone, but one had to call twice: first to request the attendant to notify loved ones to come to the phone, and second to speak to them. By 2001, Kuchmil had obtained a cellular pay phone and a CB radio. The pay phone, located in one of the small stores, had limited service due to the remoteness of the cell tower. Although cell phones were readily available and in frequent use in urban areas in 2001, their cost, like landlines, was prohibitive; migrant workers who purchased cell phones used them only for special occasions or emergencies. In contrast, the CB radio was more reliable. It was installed in the *comisaría* and was used primarily to stay in touch with municipal headquarters regarding government duties, political party obligations, or medical emergencies. Yet by 2011, these communication methods had become antiquated as cell phones and their data plans became affordable and internet access was made widely available both in Cancún and in Kuchmil. Isolation is no longer a hallmark of rural villages like Kuchmil.

Cancún and Kuchmil make up an extended social space where it is common for people to organize their lives around movement back and forth between these two places. Adolescents and young men and women spend summers in Cancún before graduating from high school or college, while migrant workers periodically return to Kuchmil to take breaks of several months to a year from the rat race in Cancún or to care for aging or ailing parents. Indeed, my ethnography of migration was inspired by the constant flow of people, goods, and money between Kuchmil and Cancún (Castellanos 2010b). This mobility also shaped Maya settlement practices in Cancún. Economic stability in Cancún is dependent on access to housing. Rents are exorbitant, consuming one month's salary. When I lived in Cancún, I paid more than half my monthly stipend to rent an apartment. Since monthly payments on a home or a plot of land are usually more reasonable, migrants diligently save toward a down payment. For Maya migrants, becoming property owners can offset the insecurity of hotel work with its short-term contracts and fluctuating tourist flows. Yet as migrants become settlers, concerns over Cancún's economic future abound.

The advent of affordable cell phone technology and wireless internet has made more visible and audible the ties that bind Kuchmil and Cancún, but it also speaks to Cancún's transformation from *provincia* (province) to translocality,[9] a process that has solidified the ethnic, class, and spatial divisions that I described earlier even as it exposed fissures that destabilize these racial and social formations. I became attuned to these ruptures via my own evolution from student to professor. When I was a doctoral student, my status as a *gringa* gave me access to politicians and government bureaucrats, but my status as a *pocha* (a Mexican American or Chicana) and a woman curtailed this access. My skin was too brown, my accent too working class, my dress and hair style not quite polished enough, for Cancún's elite to take me seriously. By 2011, the titles of doctor and professor opened new doors that made me privy to conversations marked by power and privilege or the lack thereof. People from diverse racial, ethnic, and class backgrounds shared with me their deep-held anxieties about Cancún's future and their place within it. This social angst is captured in one taxi driver's simple statement: "Cancún anda muy mal." This feeling of Cancún as having lost its way, of being on the downslide, is not new. It speaks to ongoing debates about Cancún's race relations, its development (and lack thereof), its rising drug and gang violence, and its economic instability.

This anxiety is clearly manifested in the way that people talk about migrants who are deemed less "cultured." As Cancún's international reputation has grown, so has its population. In 1971, approximately six thousand people lived in Cancún. Today close to a million people reside here. This influx of migrants has been primarily working class. In 2000, 40 percent of the migrants residing in the state of Quintana Roo hailed from the state of Yucatán, many of whom came from rural Indigenous towns (INEGI 1999, 27). As a result, racial and class ideologies, which pit Maya against Yucatecan, Mexican against Yucatecan, continue to structure interethnic relations. Over the last decade as migrant streams originating from outside the peninsula and the nation increased, new hierarchies have been reinscribed over old ones, again buttressed by ethnic, racial, and class stereotypes. Capturing this shift in power relations calls for "rethinking difference *through* connections" (Gupta and Ferguson 1992, 8; emphasis in original). For example, in the hotel industry, employers prefer Yucatecan workers because of their ascribed "strong work ethic"; migrant workers from places like Tabasco or Guatemala are considered lazy and combative. Yet outside of work, *chilangos*—residents of Mexico City—deem Yucatecans to be provincial, as less than (both less cultured and less intelligent). These stereotypes undergird labor market niches; folks from Veracruz, Tabasco, Chiapas, and Guatemala dominate the construction industry, whereas Yucatecans are concentrated in the hotel and service industries. Even within hotels, most of the women working as maids and at least half the bartenders and waiters are commonly Yucatecan. Yet the bellboys and receptionists—positions with greater prestige, income, and education requirements—typically hail from states outside of the Yucatán Peninsula and look less Indian, with fair skin or European features, than the service staff. Young men and women from Kuchmil with university degrees in tourism do not fit this idealized racial model and find it difficult to obtain jobs befitting their training and education. They end up working in housekeeping or as waiters or security guards, hoping to move from the "back" to the "front" of the hotel when a position "opens" up.

This narrative about Cancún's decline also speaks to concerns over Cancún's brand as a tourist icon. "Cancún is like Paris," hotel workers explained because, like the city of lights, it is recognized globally as a vacation getaway. In Cancún's open-air markets, tourists can buy a T-shirt that lists famous cities next to their iconic symbols: Paris and the Eiffel Tower, New York City and the Statue of Liberty, London and the London Bridge, and Cancún and the Chac Mool (a pre-Columbian stone statue). Cancún remains popular as a spring break mecca for college students. The drinking, nudity, and mayhem serve as spectacles that continually attract students, even as they have tarnished Cancún's image. Tourists I encounter, especially wealthy American tourists, often remark that Cancún is a "pit." When Hurricane Wilma devastated Cancún in October 2005 and forced two-thirds of the hotels to shut down for renovations (thus demoralizing the city's workforce, many of whom lost their jobs), the Mexican government and business community spent several billion dollars to rebuild the city. Tourism provides a critical source of revenue for a struggling national economy. This redevelopment was intended to redeem Cancún's brand by catering to boutique and ecofriendly tourism, an intentional effort to diminish the influx of "spring breakers." Within six months of the devastation, the majority of the hotels were open for business. This investment and speedy redevelopment reassured hotel workers—or at least the lucky ones with jobs—that the future of Cancún, and hence their economic futures, was fully supported by an alliance forged between the national government and transnational businesses.

But recently another side to Cancún has increasingly resembled global cities like Paris and thus merits a closer look. Although renowned as a tourist mecca and spectacle, Cancún is best described as a global metropole with its influx of transnational capital and migrant labor and its urban density and increasing class inequality. Yet popular depictions and imaginings of Cancún rely on its origin myth—a beach resort built in the midst of a sleepy Maya fishing village—thus reproducing settler colonial narratives of virgin forests and Indian authenticity. Forty years later, Cancún's population has grown exponentially, making the city one of the fastest growing in Latin America. Indeed, in 1991, when I first visited Cancún, the city retained its provincial feel. There was only one ATM where I could access money from my U.S. bank account. It was located on the main thoroughfare—Tulum Avenue—a bustling place where tourists and locals interacted while shopping for arts and crafts, sundries, and groceries, and while eating at local and foreign eateries like McDonald's. A decade later with a population of over half a million, Cancún had become an urban metropolis, attracting people outside of the Yucatán Peninsula whose business interests go beyond the scope of tourism.[10] Today this population is projected at close to one million, resulting in traffic congestion and gridlock and an influx of wealth concentrated in segregated enclaves and gated communities.

Hotels no longer seek a clientele of college students and budget travelers. Instead, wealthy tourists and ecotourists have become new, lucrative targets. Cancún's brand now hinges on the idea of luxury. This sense of leisure is directed inward as well, catering to the influx of wealth brought by new residents: Mexicans fleeing the drug war, American and Canadian snowbirds, South Americans displaced by collapsing economies, and Europeans seeking economic opportunities. In response, real estate developers have built private enclaves priced from US$250,000 and up. To meet the needs of a growing elite, universities doubled in number from the year 2000 to the year 2011.[11] Walmart, which targets tourists and the middle class in Mexico, opened an additional two stores bringing its total to three stores. Starbucks anchors many malls throughout the city. Shopping centers cater to luxurious tastes with the recent openings of the upscale Mexican department store El Palacio de Hierro and luxury designer boutiques like Louis Vuitton, Salvatore Ferragamo, and Gucci.

Real estate developers are building for the poor as well. Social housing for Cancún's working classes is intent on replacing the self-built housing of Cancún's past. After the state government halted its land redistribution program in 2001, private developers and banks, with financial subsidies from the federal government, stepped in to provide affordable housing and mortgages for the working class.[12] Funding through the Instituto del Fondo Nacional de la Vivienda para los Trabajadores (INFONAVIT, Institute of the National Housing Fund for Workers) has made this housing popular among Maya migrants. These social housing developments, many of which are located along Cancún's *periférico* (the new superhighway running along the city's northern boundary), consist of row after row of identical units, designed as townhomes or as single-family homes. On the surface this bustling metropolis may appear to have succeeded in shedding its rural origins and in transforming its migrant labor force, primarily made up of Indigenous peoples and peasants, into modern urban citizens. But the *regiones* and new housing estates remain spaces where rural Indigenous practices are invoked as models for social organizing (Castellanos 2019).

Before becoming homeowners, Maya migrants rented apartments scattered throughout the city. Where they lived was based on factors beyond their control: location, access to bus routes, cheap rent, and their relatives' generosity in providing housing. When I began dissertation work in Cancún, few migrants had time to visit each other because of their busy work schedules, which made it difficult for me to find where migrants lived. I seriously debated whether a Maya "community" existed in Cancún given these limitations. Conversely, homeownership in new developments offers the opportunity for Maya migrants to live within the same vicinity, possibly even the same neighborhood, because all the construction (at least initially) took place at the edge of town, within proximity to the neighborhoods where Maya migrants previously rented apartments. Now Maya migrants visit each other frequently, especially to celebrate rituals like the *heetzmeek* and to prepare for an upcoming *quinceañera*.[13] These ceremonies, which used to be celebrated back in Kuchmil, take place more frequently in Cancún as migrants opt to host the event in their home to avoid requesting time off from work. Now family members from Kuchmil travel to attend these events in Cancún.

These housing developments may promote community among Maya migrants, but they also generate anxiety among working-class Mexicans because they are tied to the growing financialization of life in Cancún. New credit opportunities, from credit cards to microfinance, make it possible for Cancunenses to furnish their new homes, buy new cars or scooters, and join the digital age. With the advent of social housing, thousands of Cancunenses took on mortgages that they deemed to be affordable but that in reality were not. José, a taxi driver originally from Tizimín, Yucatán, explained why he had a difficult time paying his mortgage. He purchased his apartment before the economic crisis, when he was doing well. Now even though he earns nine thousand pesos (the equivalent of 750 U.S. dollars) a month, he sometimes cannot afford to pay his monthly mortgage of 642 pesos (approximately equivalent to 53.50 U.S. dollars). "Occasionally, my mother and my kids get sick and I don't have the money to pay [the mortgage]." As in the tragic stories from the housing crash in the United States, medical expenses and the current downturn in tourism can easily bankrupt a family in Mexico. Foreclosures have become so common that housing units on the edge of town have been completely abandoned or were never occupied. The jungle is slowly creeping up on these vacant shells without doors or windows, bearing the graffiti tags of local gangs; they have become modern-day ruins to the violence of Cancún's modernity. Ties to U.S. markets as a result of NAFTA and to global markets with the expansion of tourism, consumption, and housing have made it increasingly difficult for working-class Mexicans to weather global financial crises. As the famous Mexican proverb states, when the United States catches a cold, Mexico catches pneumonia.

Rebuilding Cancún into a cosmopolitan city has also resulted in a loss of space, especially green space. Alicia, a friend who is originally from Zacatecas and has lived in Cancún for more than twenty years, shared her surprise at Cancún's growth. She spent an evening visiting a friend who purchased a luxury apartment overlooking Laguna Nichupté with a view of Cancún's skyline. When Alicia looked out of the wall-to-wall windows, she saw the city of Cancún spread out before her. "I was shocked. I felt like I was in Mexico City." To equate Cancún with one of the largest cities in the world speaks to this city's transformation on a global scale, but it also speaks to the environmental and infrastructural problems that accompany this growth. Among Cancún's older residents, complaints over the loss of Cancun's foliage and jungle are common. Unlike the recent migrants, they moved to Cancún because they were attracted by the lush forest and the provincial feel. That feeling is gone. It has been replaced with a backlash toward development projects, a sentiment that is encapsulated in critiques of the *fraccionamientos* (housing developments) by taxi drivers and the middle class. "The *fraccionamientos* are a nightmare," my friend Valentina lamented. For her, this cookie-cutter construction held very little appeal. "There are too many people from elsewhere. The people from Tabasco have arrived. What a horror. Those from Guatemala, *los chapitas* [Indigenous people from Chiapas]." A taxi driver from Veracruz proclaimed, "It's bad that they keep constructing *fraccionamientos* because many houses are empty. People could not pay so they abandoned them and returned to their villages. They should occupy those houses before they begin to build new ones and destroy more forest." While this concern is laudable and speaks to Cancunenses' longstanding commitment to environmental action, this discourse is also racialized. The lack of green space is a problem that is clearly evident throughout all of Cancún's neighborhoods, including the new wealthy enclaves built along the highway to the airport. Yet it is referenced only when speaking of development for the working class, for tourists, and for the poor.

P.S. We're Having a Great Time in Mexico!

Cancún's expansion has not diminished the feelings of hope and despair that continue to form part of the city's growing pains. Despite these trappings of wealth and an expanding middle class, Cancún's makeover was not a complete success. Upscale tourists continue to bypass Cancún for the "pristine" natural beauty of Tulum and Akumal farther south along the Riviera. A well-known Hollywood actress I met ridiculed Cancún for being too "corporate." The image of Cancún as "ugly," as "too Western," and as "lacking culture"—accusations that have been levied at some point by tourists, locals, and migrants alike to me whether I claimed to be a student, a tourist, or an anthropologist—remains pervasive. These claims form part of global critique and discourse around environmental protection and Indigenous authenticity used by a tourism industry to promote ecotourism and boutique tourism. Who is speaking for whom here?

Although I have made similar critiques of Cancún, I find myself becoming defensive whenever someone lambastes this city and its people. My travels have taught me to historicize and contextualize my critiques, whereas most tourists' comments are flippantly dismissive of a people and a culture. When an American couple with whom I spent the day complained about the presence of Walmart in Cancún, I reminded them that "Mexicans want goods too, just like Americans" and gave them a minilecture on the history of Cancún's development. For people with whom I have brief encounters, like the Hollywood actress, I stay mute because it is difficult to change deeply ingrained attitudes about Mexico in a couple of minutes. And I have only so much energy to spare. These are the moments that hurt the most because they call forth the class and racial stereotypes that continue to be perpetuated under Mexico's modernization efforts. For Cancún and the Maya Riviera to remain a top vacation destination, images of poor Indians, pristine jungle, and cheap goods must abound. For tourists to have a "good time" in Mexico means that Mexicans must hustle on a daily basis—to cater to the fickle taste of tourists, to clean hotel rooms, and to make enough money to feed their families in an economy that fluctuates seasonally and is deeply impacted by economic recessions. Hustling, my consultants remind me, is a national condition, and it keeps them, their city, and their country afloat.

Notes

1. I use pseudonyms for all rural towns and people mentioned here, with the exception of the names of public figures.
2. The term *gringo* used to refer to a foreigner of Anglo-Saxon descent from the United States, but the usage in Mexico has been broadened to include most foreigners from other nation-states, regardless of ethnicity.
3. I lived in Cancún from September 2000 through September 2001 while conducting fieldwork for my dissertation. The exchange rate fluctuated between 8.98 pesos to 10 pesos per dollar. The average exchange rate was 9.2 pesos per dollar; I use this exchange rate for the snapshot of September 2000. In 2011, the exchange rate was at 11 pesos per dollar. A *combi* ride from the airport had increased to thirteen U.S. dollars.
4. When the new international airport terminal (known as Terminal 3) was completed in 2007, a bus stop was placed outside this terminal as well. The bus to Playa del Carmen was also relocated to a stop at the new terminal.
5. For a detailed discussion of the conflict between don Dani and don Enrique, see Castellanos 2010a.
6. Maya words are spelled using the orthographic style used by the Academia Lengua Maya.
7. Hacienda owners and town residents with Spanish surnames abandoned the region or were killed during the Caste War (1847–1901), the most successful Indian insurrection in Mesoamerica. See Reed 2001.
8. The dialogues between foreigners and Yucatec Maya people are well documented. In the *Incidents of Travel in Yucatan*, John Lloyd Stephens (1843) wrote about his experience searching for ancient Maya sites and talking with the descendants of these city-states. In the early 1900s, the Carnegie Institution of Washington funded a series of studies in the Yucatán Peninsula that resulted in works by Sylvanus Morley (1913), Robert Redfield and Alfonso Villa Rojas ([1934] 1990),

Ralph L. Roys (1957), and Morris Steggerda (1941), among others. For an analysis of the relationships forged through these encounters, see Paul Sullivan 1991 and Quetzil E. Castañeda 1996.

9.   Arjun Appadurai (1996, 192) offers a definition of translocality: "locations [that] create complex conditions for the production and reproduction of locality, in which ties of marriage, work, business, and leisure weave together various circulating populations with kinds of locals to create neighborhoods that belong in one sense to particular nation-states, but that are from another point of view what we might call *translocalities*" (emphasis in original). I adopt this term to refer to places that engage with a transnational flow of goods, people, money, and ideas.

10. In 2010, the municipality of Benito Juárez included 661,176 residents. Although the bulk of these residents lived in Cancún, this number included population tallies for the smaller localities of Alfredo V. Bonfil, Puerto Morelos, Leona Vicario, Puerto Juaréz, and Central Vallarta. See INEGI 2011.

11. The Instituto Tecnológico de Cancún, which opened in 1984, was the first university established in Cancún. It was followed by the Universidad La Salle Cancún (1991), the Universidad Tecnológica de Cancún (1998), the Universidad Anáhuac Cancún (2000), the Universidad del Caribe (2000), the Universidad Magna (2002), and the TecMilenio (2006, on the campus of the Universidad Magna). Since then, additional universities have been established, such as the Universidad Interamericana para el Desarrollo, Universidad Politécnica de Quintana Roo, Escuela Superior de Leyes, Universidad Maya de las Américas, Universidad Internacional de Estuidos Superiores, and Universidad Aliat-Latinoamericana de Quintan Roo.

12. For a discussion and critique of the state's land redistribution program, see Castellanos 2008.

13. The *heetzmeek* and *quinceañera* celebrate particular stages in a child's life. The *heetzmeek* (straddle-hip) ceremony is performed to awaken an infant's faculties and to designate godparents who will help guide the child's religious education and future development. The *quinceañera* celebrates a girl's fifteenth birthday.

References

Anzaldúa, Gloria. 1987. *Borderlands/La Frontera: The New Mestiza*. San Francisco: Aunt Lute Books.

Appadurai, Arjun. 1996. *Modernity at Large: Cultural Dimensions of Globalization*. Minneapolis: University of Minnesota Press.

Castañeda, Quetzil E. 1996. *In the Museum of Maya Culture: Touring Chichén Itzá*. Minneapolis: University of Minnesota Press.

Castellanos, M. Bianet. 2008. "Constructing the Family: Mexican Migrant Households, Marriage, and the State." *Latin American Perspectives* 35 (1): 64–77.

Castellanos, M. Bianet. 2010a. "Don Teo's Expulsion: Property Regimes, Moral Economies, and Ejido Reform." *Journal of Latin American and Caribbean Anthropology* 15 (1): 144–69.

Castellanos, M. Bianet. 2010b. *A Return to Servitude: Maya Migration and the Tourist Trade in Cancún*. Minneapolis: University of Minnesota Press.

Castellanos, M. Bianet. 2019. "L'invocation du bien commun: Les migrants mayas, le logement et les squatteurs au Méxique" [Invoking the commons: Maya migrants, housing, and squatter settlements in Mexico]. *Anthropologie et Sociétés* 43 (2): forthcoming.

Elmendorf, Mary. 1976. *Nine Mayan Women*. Cambridge, Mass.: Schenkman Books.

Gupta, Akhil, and James Ferguson. 1992. "Beyond 'Culture': Space, Identity, and the Politics of Difference." *Cultural Anthropology* 7 (1): 6–23.

INEGI (Instituto Nacional Estadístico, Geográfico e Informático). 1999. *Encuesta Nacional de la Dinámica Demográfica 1997: Panorama Sociodemográfico Quintana Roo*. Mexico City: INEGI.

INEGI (Instituto Nacional Estadístico, Geográfico e Informático). 2011. *Principales Resultados del Censo de Población y Vivienda 2010, Quintana Roo*. Mexico City: INEGI.

Morley, Sylvanus. 1913. "Archaeological Research at the Ruins of Chichen Itza, Yucatan." In *Reports upon the Present Condition and Future Needs of the Science of Anthropology*, Carnegie Institution of Washington publication no. 200, by W. H. R. Rivers, Albert E. Jenks, and Sylvanus G. Morley, 61–91. Washington, D.C.: Carnegie Institution of Washington.

Re Cruz, Alicia. 1996. *The Two Milpas of Chan Kom*. Albany: State University of New York Press.

Redfield, Robert, and Alfonso Villa Rojas. (1934) 1990. *Chan Kom: A Maya Village*. Prospect Heights, Ill.: Waveland Press.

Reed, Nelson. 2001. *The Caste War of Yucatán*. Stanford, Calif.: Stanford University Press.

Roys, Ralph L. 1957. *The Political Geography of the Yucatán Maya*. Washington, D.C.: Carnegie Institution of Washington.

Steggerda, Morris. 1941. *Maya Indians of Yucatan*. Washington, D.C.: Carnegie Institution of Washington.

Stephens, John Lloyd. 1843. *Incidents of Travel in Yucatan*. Washington, D.C.: Smithsonian Books.

Sullivan, Paul. 1991. *Unfinished Conversations: Mayas and Foreigners Between Two Wars*. Berkeley: University of California Press.

SIX

Selling Affect, Seeking Blood

The Economy of Pain at El Mozote, El Salvador

ELLEN MOODIE AND LEIGH BINFORD

The bayonet stops them. Again and again, almost hearing it slice the air, the visitors catch their breath.[1]

This day they are listening to Raquel Márquez, a slender, soft-spoken young woman. For the past six years, she has been leading tours of her birthplace, the hamlet of El Mozote in northeastern El Salvador—the site of the largest massacre in modern Latin American history. This particular tour comprises a small group of Catholics who have traveled from Sacred Heart Church in Illinois.[2] They have just finished their annual visit to their *hermanamiento* (sister community) La Cruz, a few hours east over mountain roads. Raquel is one of several women waiting when the Illinoisans arrive that overcast day in July 2011. She approaches them tentatively as they disembark from their truck onto the cobblestoned plaza facing a small stone, mortar, and metal monument, which commemorates the carnage of thirty years ago. They introduce themselves to her—four parishioners and a priest, along with anthropologist Ellen Moodie.

Raquel announces that the story she is about to share comes directly from Rufina Amaya (who died in 2007), "the only survivor of the [El Mozote] massacre."[3] In the refugee camps of Colomoncagua, Honduras, where many people from the area fled afterward, she says, Amaya inspired her fellow refugees to examine publicly what had happened during those three days in December 1981. Today her testimony is one of the key references of the twelve-year conflict that was the Salvadoran Civil War. Often called one of the last battles of the Cold War, the war pitted leftist guerrillas of the Farabundo Martí National Liberation Front (FMLN) against the U.S.-supported Salvadoran government. It began in 1980 and ended after the United Nations brokered peace accords in 1992. The FMLN became a political party and in 2009, after almost two decades of right-wing rule, won the presidency.

Raquel walks the group to the front of the monument, a black metal sculpture cut into the silhouette of a mother, father, and two children.[4] Behind it is a copper wall covered with plaques listing victims, whole families of them. The surnames repeat again and again: Argueta, Chicas, Claros, Díaz, Márquez, Romero.

She begins her narration. She metes out her tale in fluid bits, pausing for translation after each sentence.

"Rufina Amaya says that on the eleventh of December, they [the army] called together all of the people.

"They began to form groups. The women were massacred in that house over there, the house of Israel Márquez, the leader of the community. The children were massacred in the rose garden [next to the church] . . .

"The men were massacred in the house of Alfredo Márquez.

"They made the women line up, a line of twenty-two women. Rufina Amaya was the last, because she was fighting with a soldier—that they not take an eight-month-old girl from her.

"Rufina Amaya tells us that they took her girl from her, and they threw her up [into the air] and then waited for the baby to fall, with a double-edged knife.

"She fainted."

A beat passes.

No one speaks.

No one breathes.

Shannon, an Irish-American historian and new parishioner at Sacred Heart, converts Raquel's gentle Salvadoran Spanish into crisp classroom U.S. English. She is practiced by now, after translating homilies of the priest, Father Dan, into Spanish in daily masses offered in La Cruz over the past week. Her voice is solemn, as if to avoid any affect.

"They tore the baby from her," Shannon tells the group. "They threw it up into the air, and they impaled it with a bayonet. She fainted." Her words bend slightly Raquel's narration, which leaves the soldiers waiting below the infant's body without describing the descent.

We need to hear specifics, Shannon will say that night over hot chocolate, when Ellen asks her what she thinks of Raquel's words. That is part of what *compels* us to go to El Mozote, she insists: the massive and spectacular violence. We can't travel all that way to a remote hamlet in the middle of Central America and then hide (from) the whole truth. We must make what happened visible. Even if we flinch. Especially if some still deny it. Ellen agrees, uneasily. She still wonders how to think about our desire to see (or hear about) blood upon blood.

And yet Ellen also recognizes that this same blood first compelled her to go to El Salvador, as an activist, and then to return, again and again, as an anthropologist. As if anthropology could absolve her. Blood soaked the earliest stories she heard about El Salvador as a college student in the 1980s, listening to refugees' testimonies at the Indiana University campus, reading the *New York Times*. Blood paid for by the United States government. She signed petitions, protested, and then finally went herself to see, in 1993, after the war ended. Her returns feel compulsive, especially as El Salvador has come back to global attention as a site of trauma. Are we so different, tourists, priests, activists, anthropologists?

In this chapter, we examine what might be called a tourist economy of pain, in which what *sells* is blood—memory of (or imagining of) blood. We do not question that pain and suffering should be remembered and commemorated. But we wonder at the *effects* of selling *affect* among tourists. Local tour guides in El Mozote and other sites of horror, especially those identified with a massacre, often perform a kind of emotion work—whether as a relative of a victim or simply as a resident of a place known for conflict—as they recount histories (Hochschild 1979). How does the economic pressure of tourism shape or even distort the very history that has produced the place as a tourist attraction?

Raquel continues her tour of El Mozote, pointing to the hill where young girls were taken and raped before being killed. She describes how the soldiers set the corpses on fire, leaving charred bodies across the central plaza and among the burned buildings.

Father Dan later asks, through Shannon, how many died that day. Raquel has a ready answer—she wields precise statistics. A total of 420 children, 160 adults, and six "elderly people." Dan nods. "Mostly children," he says, turning to his parishioners.[5]

The events that Raquel describes in the *caserio* (hamlet) of El Mozote were part of a series of attacks considered part of the same massacre. The three-day scorched-earth campaign was executed by the Atlacatl Battalion, one of five

U.S.-trained special combat units. Most accounts today estimate that soldiers strangled, stabbed, shot, and then burned more than a thousand people, mostly women, children, and elderly males.[6]

On that December day more than thirty years ago, after being forced into line by the soldiers, the survivor Rufina Amaya found herself obscured between a small crab-apple tree and a pine tree. She had fallen to her knees in despair, begging God to forgive her sins. Either that or she purposefully turned and threw herself behind a tree, hiding from her captors. The soldiers were distracted by the terrified cries of women at the front of the line and did not see her. Different published versions of her testimony suggest both possibilities. The distinction is not insignificant; the first implies relinquishment of control and capitulation to inevitable death, the second involves a desperate but willful act to escape it.[7] In her soft narration of Rufina's story that July afternoon, Raquel does not mention the crab-apple tree. Rather she says that Rufina decided to hide among the cattle. But before she crawled away, Raquel says, Rufina heard her children's cries. "She crouched down, and she began to hear the screams. She could hear her own children calling out to her. 'Mamá Rufina, they're killing us! Mamá Rufina, they're killing us!'"

By the time that she died in March 2007, Rufina Amaya had repeated her testimony dozens, probably hundreds, of times, to villagers who hid with her in a cave soon after the massacre, to news reporters, to international human-rights observers and officials, to her fellow refugees in Honduras, to judges, to anthropologists and activists, and finally to delegations such as this group of Illinois Catholics. Indeed, for a good part of the 1990s, she had shared her story with other members of Sacred Heart, each time weeping, until Father Dan could not bear to see her repeat it again. "We would meet her after visiting El Mozote, in a café in Perquín [a nearby town], and people could ask her questions," he explained to me later. "Sometimes she would bring her daughter Martita [born after the massacre]. That was nice. Life goes on."

In July 2011, Father Dan, now in his mid-seventies and partially deaf, listens intently, although he knows the chronology well. He has returned to the site several dozen times since his first trip in January 1992. Later, though, as we sit in the double-cabin pickup truck on our way back to the Posada El Torogoz in nearby Jocoaitique, he will agree with me and John, a delegation member who is a peace activist and occasional Sacred Heart parishioner. Never, in all the times that Rufina Amaya recited her story, nor in all the published versions, have any of us heard of a knife lancing a child tossed into the air.

It is a gruesome vision. Evil and innocence merge in a flash. It testifies to unfathomable cruelty. The image, an infant pierced like a pig on a spit, condenses the horror of so many stories people have heard about the Salvadoran Civil War: death squads leaving decapitated bodies of union activists on the side of the roads near San Salvador, their heads on pikes dotting the nearby fields. Peasants in Chalatenango, another war-torn department, machine-gunned by both Honduran and Salvadoran troops as they fled a military operation, trying to cross the flowing Sumpul River and escape to Honduras.

Ellen in fact heard a version of the baby and the bayonet story a year earlier, from another guide and with a different delegation from the Illinois church—though not in relation to Rufina Amaya. The group went to a small cafeteria after the tour. As they began to eat their *pupusas* (tortillas filled with meat, cheese, or beans), one of the members, a young doctor, suddenly got up, nauseous, and left the restaurant. After vomiting she spent the next hour sitting on the sidewalk, weeping softly. Later she would explain that she could not shake the image of that one child's crude slaughter.

Is it true? Is it a fragment of experience that Rufina Amaya could not bear to say aloud for so long, not to sympathetic international visitors, nor to human-rights lawyers from the capital? Is it something that she finally confessed to a small group of kinswomen—whispering to victims' relatives like Raquel Márquez? Or is it simply the guides' embellishment, a vivid image conjured to sensationalize the events in the economy of pain—satisfying at least foreign tourists' desires for high drama, and possibly extracting a few more coins from them?[8]

As anthropologists who study violence, who interpret human-rights discourses, we might stop ourselves and ask: Why quibble with possible inaccuracies? After all, anthropologists, too, sometimes embellish the stories they recount, or they select the provocative account from among a mass of mundane ones as they transact exchanges with readers, their anthropological subjects serving as a raw material of mediation. Readers "tour" the domain of the Other in the wake of the anthropologist-guide.

Indeed, Rufina Amaya wasn't the only survivor of the massacre at El Mozote (even the earliest reports show that others escaped death too). And she probably didn't hear her own children's cries. Her escape, the very fact of her survival, was not something she could fully explain. But what does it matter? She got away. More than a thousand died: her children, her partner, her compadres and friends, her world. Who, in the end, in a ninety-minute visit, can take the time to tell the "whole" story—as if it were possible to account with precision the years of poverty and deprivation through the twentieth century and the long, slow story of the U.S.-supported anti-Communist campaigns that led to the twelve-year-long civil war in which at least seventy-five thousand people died?

Is telling a condensed, partly imagined terror easier than revealing the deeply felt personal experience of people who are still alive? It could be that this powerful image, the bayonet impaling the infant, captures violent excess in a way that dry bones reassembled by forensic anthropologists, or lists of names of victims carved into a polished marble wall, cannot. Perhaps only fiction can adequately express what happened. At the same time, there can be no question that a massacre of a thousand-plus women, children, and elderly people surpasses any military determination to suppress insurgents.

* * *

We believe that exploring the way that events are narrated in tourist visits at the El Mozote historical site can help us think about what is exchanged in this tourist economy of pain—in the transaction between visitors to sites of human-rights violations and people who lived through, or close to, atrocities. Certainly the simple, linear accounts offered (for voluntary donations) to busloads of tourists can garble historical memory. The demands of listeners from the Global North or other parts of the world—their very passport-stamped presence affirming unequal power relations to Salvadorans, especially those in northern Morazán—might lead to the preference for some kinds of narratives over others.[9] Such processes might well further silence already difficult recollections, especially those that veer from a sheen of innocence versus evil. Some might argue that such clamoring for simple subtleties to translate a complicated history is even dangerous.

Consider the right-wing campaign to discredit Guatemalan Nobel Peace Prize laureate Rigoberta Menchú, after anthropologist David Stoll (1999) challenged parts of her *testimonio* (the account of her life of struggle and resistance; see Menchú and Burgos-Debray 1987). In that case, Stoll learned that some of the things that Menchú had said about key historical events, including the torture and murder of her brother, did not reflect what others had seen and could not be corroborated. An enormous debate ensued about Western scholarship and indigenous ways of thinking, about *testimonio* as a form of urgent storytelling, and about truth and relativity. Questions of history and memory, of the forms of framing and even packaging experience for outsiders, remain potent (Arias 2001).

Must the commodification of history in this economy of pain equal forgetting, erasure (Huyssen 2003, 21–22)? Or could the presence of outsiders, eager for a flash of the past with their digital cameras and recorders, contribute to emancipatory possibilities for the emergence of social memory? After all, memory itself is "transitory, notoriously unreliable, and haunted by forgetting," ever subject to change, as literary critic Andreas Huyssen (2003, 28) puts it. Perhaps, like miniature simulacra of the war-era Central American solidary *testimonio*, the questions, conversations, and even the confusion that others bring into the site of trauma can contribute to new ways of reflecting on experience, to narrating the past—and, as such, to acting in history (Trouillot 1995, 24).

But there is a darker reading of the relationships that unfold at these sites across the world (from concentration camps in Poland to Ground Zero in New York), one in which tourists seek out blood, death, and destruction, and guides and others feed these desires by portraying events in gruesome detail (Lennon and Foley 2000). At El Mozote, the image of impaled infants, or, as Leigh recorded in June 2012, guides' accounts of children's bodies hung by soldiers like Christmas ornaments from a tree near the church, stand as two such invented accounts. Why would sightseers desire such images? Is the murder of a thousand men, women, and children not sufficient?

Many Salvadorans tour El Mozote, too, of course. It is a four-hour drive from the capital by car, a longer bus ride. The cool, pine-covered mountains in this area near the Honduran border draw people seeking a break from the tropical heat below. Hundreds of schoolchildren and university students take buses each year to this remote corner of the country. Their knowledge of their own history possibly exceeds that of the foreign tourist (though a number of foreign travelers, especially from the solidarity movement, have studied the war). And while the massacre at El Mozote has become iconic of war terror, few Salvadorans, especially young ones, know much more than the rudimentary outlines.

Take what happened in August 2011, when Ellen joined a group of Salvadoran tourists for the annual winter festival on a five-hour hike from Perquín over a small mountain to El Mozote. The trek was led by Father Rogelio Ponceele, a Belgian cleric who had ministered to the insurgent troops as well as to the people living in this part of the country during the war. As he does every year, he paused periodically during the hike to tell the participants about his own experience in the war and the years leading up to it, as well as the events surrounding the massacre. Father Ponceele did not tell Rufina's story (and he certainly did not mention anything like the bayonet and the baby); he told a much broader political account of the origins of the conflict, rooting it in inequality. Many of the young Salvadorans there that August day were sympathetic to the FMLN, the former guerrilla force turned leftist political party. On this trip, they did not respond with surprise at atrocities—they may or may not have known many of the details of the El Mozote massacre, but they were most likely quite familiar with the cruelty carried out in the name of the nation during the 1980s. During pauses on the hike, Salvadorans lined up to take smiling selfies with the famous "guerrilla priest." He obliged jovially. But he ended the trip with a pointed reminder that this ramble was not just about long-past history: he told them that the Inter-American Court of Human Rights in San José, Costa Rica, had just accepted a petition filed by family members of El Mozote victims, charging the Salvadoran state with violating the human rights to life, personal integrity, private life, and private property, as well as the rights of children.[10]

Thirty-plus years ago, outsiders, in the form of U.S. military advisers who trained the battalion that carried out the murders, crucially shaped the brutality at El Mozote. Today, could it be, at least in part, that the involvement of other outsiders—the kindness of strangers, perhaps, but also the friction-filled misunderstandings of foreigners—is playing a key role in the gathering of local historical memory, even if through the medium of tourism's "staged authenticity" (MacCannell 1999, 97)? Often only in front of tourists, whether Salvadoran or Swedish, does a public version of history emerge in this marginalized community, so far from the cultural, commercial, and political centers of El Salvador. This emergent and living version would be one that incorporates individual stories into a shared narrative that speaks to collective experience (much as Menchú's testimony did for many in the Guatemalan Mayan community more than thirty years ago). As Florence E. Babb (2011, 2) notes, ambivalently, in her research on tourism in the postconflict and postrevolutionary sites of Cuba, Nicaragua, Mexico, and Peru, "Tourism often takes up where social transformation leaves off."[11]

* * *

The events that became known as the El Mozote massacre occurred between December 11 and 13, 1981. It was the largest of at least a dozen such army attacks in the zone during the months leading up to it (Binford [1996] 2016). The massacre encompassed six widely scattered hamlets, but the greatest loss of life took place in the center of El Mozote itself, perhaps because, as one story has it, the army forewarned the residents of the operation and passed word through the grapevine that those who concentrated in the village center would have their lives respected. This action is likely what Raquel Márquez refers to when she says, "They called together all of the people." She never clarifies the referent for the pronoun *they* in the story that she tells the tourists. She does not mention the military unit that carried out the massacre, or its U.S. connection; like most of the El Mozote guides, she tells a story that is strikingly depoliticized. The political story is told in other forums, including in tours given by ex-combatants in the Museum of the Revolution in Perquín. The hamlet El Mozote in fact had been known for staunch conservatism—Joaquín Villalobos, a guerrilla commander, would later tell journalist Mark Danner (1994, 18) that the people of El Mozote "would not support us."[12] But the army uniformly regarded the area as a "red zone" of Communist control, in part, perhaps, because El Mozote lay only a few kilometers' walk from the rebels' principal base in La Guacamaya. The army considered everyone there, apparently even eight-month-old babies, to be rebel supporters.

The particulars of the massacre have been amply discussed by journalists and scholars. Former guerrilla and journalist Carlos Henríquez Consalvi ("Santiago," the voice of the clandestine guerrilla Radio Venceremos) was the first of a long list to interview Rufina Amaya. Two weeks after the massacre he broadcast her account throughout El Salvador, along with those of other survivors (Henríquez Consalvi 2010, 82–83; 1992, 107–8). Six weeks after the event, in late January 1982, Raymond Bonner of the *New York Times* and Alma Guillermoprieto, for the *Washington Post*, would report the massacre and describe Rufina Amaya's testimony for a U.S. audience. These reports generated fierce responses from Salvadoran and U.S. officials, denying both the extent of the "alleged atrocities" and attempting to debunk the representations of victims as innocent bystanders. The officials' tactics seemed to be effective for a time. As Danner (1994, 7) put it, "For eleven years, Rufina Amaya Márquez had served the world as the most eloquent witness of what had happened at El Mozote, but though she had told her story again and again, much of the world had refused to believe her."

Danner visited El Mozote in November 1992, interviewing key actors and recording his impressions. He meticulously documented U.S. attempts to cover up the incident. A year and a half earlier, during the war, Leigh had begun fieldwork in northern Morazán, researching a social history of the community that would counter its residents' images as anonymous victims. The resulting books (Danner 1994; Binford [1996] 2016) occasionally can be seen tucked into the backpacks of some of the thousands of tourists that now visit the restored central plaza of El Mozote each year. Both accounts, translated into Spanish, have sold well in El Salvador.

These accounts tell us that the Atlacatl Battalion, the first Immediate Reaction Infantry Battalion (BIRI), trained in early 1981 by U.S. Army Special Forces instructors, marched down the main road into El Mozote after being transported into Perquín in helicopters. Soldiers rounded up the men. They locked them overnight in the church and took them out the next morning to be shot in small groups. Forensic evidence allowed scientists to construct a plausible scenario in which a few women and many children were herded in small groups into a small, one-room, adobe-walled and tile-roofed sacristy located next to the church and shot through the windows and doorway. A team of Argentine forensic anthropologists who excavated the remains of the seventeen-by-twenty-two-foot building—which by 1993 had been reduced by the elements to a mound of dirt covered with vegetation—discovered the remains of at least 143 persons among which were seven adults and 136 children with an average age of six years.

In testimony given to journalist Thomas Long and published in El Salvador in the book *Luciernagas en El Mozote* (*Fireflies in El Mozote*; Amaya, Danner, and Henríquez Consalvi 1996), Rufina Amaya describes how, after crawling away on her stomach, she hid in abandoned houses for a week, dressing herself in old clothes that she found in one house. Then she heard the voices of people whom she knew and revealed herself to them. They brought her to the cave where they had been staying—one of many hiding places in the mountains and ravines of northern Morazán that peasants used during battles. One of the women there had lost two of her children, Rufina said, and they wept together.[13] Radio Venceremos's Santiago, a Venezuelan-born *internacionalista* who had come to Central America in the mid-1970s for the revolutions, would carry out his interview with her a week later.

* * *

A few years after January 1982, when the El Mozote massacre briefly became major news in the U.S. press, John, one of the Sacred Heart delegation members in the July 2011 trip, began meeting Central Americans and learning about U.S.

involvement in El Salvador.[14] In that visit to El Mozote led by Raquel Márquez, John's knowledge and engagement exceeded that of the other parishioners. The historian/translator Shannon, who was like John in her late forties, had participated in the 1980s solidarity movement, but her academic expertise was Mexico. The other participants included Noni and Emily, recent college graduates with vague ideas about the Global South and imperialism. Both of them held a sentimental attachment to La Cruz after years of listening to Father Dan's homilies, so often full of references to El Salvador.

In a conversation months after the trip, John described to Ellen the trajectory of his interest in El Salvador: after an apolitical youth spent in suburban Chicago, he had drifted to Los Angeles, where he discovered the Catholic Worker movement, a pacifist set of communities founded in the 1930s, committed to living in voluntary poverty and to attending to the margins of society—to the homeless, refugees, and nonconformists.[15] "And you know I learned about the massacres [in El Salvador], borderline genocide, and I couldn't understand it," he said. "You know it was like I was just innocent and naïve and not willing to accept that there would be this sort of, kind of, you know, mass murder, [that it] could be intentional. It's got to be some kind of accident or some kind of side consequence."

By the early 1990s he had accepted the United States', and his own, complicity in such events. He began to participate in demonstrations at the School of the Americas in Fort Benning, Georgia, and in Washington, D.C. One day, in front of the Pentagon, someone handed him a cross. "It had the name of a one-year-old on it. Teresita de Jesús Argueta from El Salvador." He pronounced the name slowly.

> Her name across and El Salvador down. It was this white cross. I'm looking at it, and she was, she was one of the children who was killed in the El Mozote massacre. So I was, was feeling somehow responsible. . . . By virtue of my ignorance, you know what I kind of failed to do, in terms of speaking out. . . . I would reflect on this one-year-old and my relationships with people in Central and South America, people that were, you know, had confronted the sort of the horror and the consequences of U.S. policy. And to be able to interact with them and engage with them was for me in some ways an experience of God.

Years passed before John traveled to El Salvador. He had tried to teach himself Spanish, but when he finally got there he could understand very little beyond

Shannon's translations. He said that he felt disconnected, and embarrassed, as a large, white, incompetent foreigner, among the people of La Cruz, Sacred Heart's sister community. But when they got to El Mozote, he sought Teresita's name on the memorial monument and on the wall on the side of the church, where the victims and their ages are listed. By then, he said, he had come to peace with Teresita. During the tour he simply listened as Raquel spoke and Shannon translated.

John, in his (frustrated) desire to relate to Salvadorans, is in many ways typical of the engaged tourist celebrated in recent travel literature. "The apparent buzzword is *experiential*," Florence E. Babb (2011, 175; emphasis in original) writes, "and the quest is for meaning." Indeed, north–south air routes to Central America are frequently clogged with groups of well-meaning—or meaning-questing—travelers: teenagers on résumé-bolstering service trips, perhaps helping out in an orphanage in Guatemala; solidarity travelers seeking the ragged remains of revolution, whether in San Cristobal de las Casas, Mexico, or in Granada, Nicaragua; short-term missioners setting up transitory medical clinics or building wells in San Pedro Sula, Honduras.[16]

Ellen had long been skeptical of these masses of enthusiastic travelers as she encountered more and more of them on flights to the United States after yet another stay in El Salvador. In her brief conversations, she sensed the reproduction of an us/them binary precisely in the moment that people were trying to overcome distance (Howell 2009). Yet getting to know people like John, Shannon, and Father Dan, she began to recognize something more than flat caricatures of tourists looking for postcard-replication moments to catch with their digital cameras. The scholar Melani McAlister (2008, 878) points to a striking intensity of longing for connection with the world among contemporary Christians who travel on short-term missions. She finds among them an "enchanted internationalism," a historically located "feeling-practice," or "an orientation, a stance toward others and an expectation for the self." This yearning for authenticity also shapes much nonreligious volunteer and service tourism, of course. "All tourists desire [a] deeper involvement with society and culture to some degree," Dean MacCannell (1999, 10) writes. "It is a basic component of their motivation to travel." Thus these kinds of expectations also shape visitors' disappointment, when "Natives" don't look like travelers think they should—and when demonstrations of suffering are not as dramatic as anticipated.

During our returns to El Salvador over more than two decades, we have seen many such groups of religious, solidarity, or service tourists. Ellen has been traveling for years to the capital, exploring experiences with postwar crime and political expression and activism. Leigh has been focused on the historical and contemporary political economy of northern Morazán. We were both drawn to El Salvador in solidarity during the war; our (late-war and) postwar research unraveled any remnant expectations of simple binaries among Salvadorans themselves. It took longer to recognize that tourists are equally complicated in their motivations and expectations. During the summers of 2010 and 2011, we had the chance to observe many tourists when Leigh led several researchers in carrying out fieldwork among former guerrilla combatants and their supporters in northern Morazán, including El Mozote. The more prosperous visitors to this former "rebel stronghold" passed through our local base in the Perkin Lenka, a rustic ecohotel run by a burly expat from Delaware (Brenneman 2013).

In summer 2010, there were the twenty or thirty Methodists from Dallas, led by a professor of religion with kind eyes, who told us that they split time between a Catholic school in a poor San Salvador neighborhood and a spot in the Philippines (several missioners were Filipino). There were the boisterous middle schoolers from Cambridge, Massachusetts, many Latinx and African American, who had spent a week shadowing students in rural San José Las Flores, Chalatenango, their sister community.[17] There was the large, diverse collection of media studies majors from San Francisco State University, seemingly all in skinny jeans and loose black sweaters, who had landed in Morazán as part of a course charged with making some kind of public service video about natural disaster prevention.

Members of the Sacred Heart delegations do not stay in the more expensive Perkin Lenka.[18] Over the course of nearly twenty years of visits, they usually spent nights on hammocks hung in homes of La Cruz residents and ended their yearly trips with a day-long tour of the area around Perquín.[19] Sacred Heart began its relationship with El Salvador in the early 1980s, when it participated in the Sanctuary movement to protect Central American refugees (Coutin 1993). As Father Dan describes it, they were inspired by the example of martyred Salvadoran Archbishop Óscar Romero—today known as "San Romero of the Americas" after his 2018 canonization—who was assassinated while saying mass in March 1980. Dan had long been a Catholic radical, booted from one parish for his opposition to the Vietnam War. By the late 1980s, the Sacred Heart priest and parishioners made the decision to reach out directly to Central Americans as "the next step, beyond the local." Around that time, he says, he first read Rufina Amaya's testimony. In 1990 he traveled with a translator to Morazán in order to meet people in the church's *hermanamiento*, La Cruz, with whom the parish had been matched by a liberation theology–linked organization. Organized communities often sought out the help of international supporters, a practice that continues today. When Father Dan first went there, northern Morazán was still under guerrilla control; the trip was risky but also felt urgent to him.

Much like John, as well as Ellen, Father Dan felt deeply complicit with U.S. involvement in the Salvadoran War. John, we saw, had personal meditations with the name and figure of one-year-old Teresita de Jesús Argueta. Father Dan tried to come to terms with his responsibility through the people in La Cruz. In an interview, he told Ellen that during one of the earliest delegations, he asked them for forgiveness:

> I proposed to the people that they forgive us the North Americans for what we had done to them. And if they would give me their forgiveness, I would bring it back with me. No one paid attention to me! But it was a ritual of expressing my sense of sin, of my community up north, that empire that has been crushing the hopes of people for years. And so I let it be known in each of the settlements and people came forward and surrounded me and laid their hands on my head, and I knelt on the ground there, and I just let it happen.

His feelings of guilt had become acute during his first visit to El Mozote, he said. He went to the massacre site just before the peace accords were signed, in early January 1992, passing through military checkpoints to get there. He still keeps the child's shoe that he said he found among the weeds that day.

* * *

When Raquel Márquez first pauses during her July 2011 tour of El Mozote, asking for questions, Father Dan shares some of his experiences with her, nudging Shannon to translate. "I first came here in January of 1992. We came into El Mozote, which was abandoned, completely abandoned."

Raquel looks at him and smiles. "Yes, because we were the first family that returned, forty of us together. I was small, but I remember. In 1992. The reason we came was we were selling food to the scientists [the Argentine Forensic Anthropology Team (EAAF), which arrived in October 1992]."

Father Dan's voice picks up speed. "In January it was abandoned. There was a woman we picked up in Arambala [a nearby town], she came to explain things to us. She said people avoided this place because they thought it was haunted. By the time we came back in August they were beginning the forensic work here."

Raquel recalls what she saw when she, at age eleven, arrived with her family in 1992: "There wasn't anything here then. There were only coyotes who howled. I didn't even know that there were remains here. We lived in the canton Ranchería [a nearby small community in which people were also massacred in December 1981]."

She returns to the more impersonal tour mode, through Shannon's voice: "After the massacre, people went to nearby towns. The army went to burn houses and homes, so people left. They [the military] didn't care if people were inside. They did it, because Col. Domingo Monterrosa gave the order. What he wanted was that there wasn't even a seed left, that's what he said."

Father Dan wants to know more about Raquel. "Had your family lived here before?" he asks. "You were returning [to El Mozote] when you came, when the forensic anthropologists were here?"

"Yes," Raquel says. "I'm from the Márquez family. I lost six uncles and an aunt who was six months pregnant. After she was killed, they put a stone on her stomach."

After a small pause, Dan responds with another story of a visit: "One year we were here, there was an old campesino who came in here and he told us his story. I remember his name was José Socorro Chicas."

"José Socorro Chicas," Raquel says. "I'm also related—I'm Márquez Chicas . . ."

"He was an old man."

"He's still alive. He lives down there below."

"Actually his story was in the *New York Times* with a picture.[20] But he came down to tell us his story, too. . . . When the situation became very troubled, he and his wife went to live with relatives, I think in Santa Tecla."

"Mm hmm."

"And many of his grandchildren were among the victims."

"Yes, my grandfather, too, he's from the same family, my grandfather lost seventeen grandchildren."

"Well, I think maybe it's the same one, because he mentioned that in order to grieve for his dead grandchildren . . ." Father Dan pauses, unable to speak for a moment. "He came, and the bones were close to the surface . . . there were wild dogs. . . . So he collected the bones, sixteen, the same number as his grand-children, he collected them and brought them home, in order to remember his grandchildren. To grieve them."

"It's the same person," Raquel says softly.

Father Dan returns to his first visit. "We were here in early January 1992, and of course they had had a memorial service for the [tenth] . . . year of the assassination. We saw bits of lit candles in the service. Otherwise the place was abandoned, weeds up to their knees."

Raquel says no more. She walks the group into the rose garden, planted in memory of the victims next to the church. "This is where the children were killed," she says quietly. She points to the church wall. "These are the names and ages of [the murdered] children." John walks over to read the names. Shannon and Raquel talk in a corner, while Father Dan explains to Noni and Emily, who nod dutifully, how the massacre was covered in the U.S. press. He recites how Congressman Thomas P. "Tip" O'Neill led a resolution to demand human-rights reports from the government of El Salvador, reports that in his view were never really effective.[21]

Shannon will later tell the delegation what she learned from Raquel. When the massacre happened, Raquel's mother had been pregnant with her—but at that moment she was at work in another part of the country, harvesting coffee beans. "So that's how they survived," Shannon explains.

The tour ends in a small cinder block structure, where the women's collective sells small items—woven purses, scarves, embroidered blouses, printed T-shirts, key chains, CDs of revolutionary music. Raquel shows the group a book with photographs taken by Radio Venceremos's Santiago soon after the massacre. She asks for "voluntary donations" that she stresses are for grounds upkeep. She then quickly leaves. Shannon, Noni, and Emily browse quietly, purchasing a few small items.

Father Dan turns to the women working in the shop. He asks about another survivor of the massacre, Andrea, who could never talk about what happened.

One of them answers Father Dan in a defiant voice. "It isn't easy," she tells him (through Ellen's translation).

Every day remembering the story, remembering the suffering that we lived. Because we, we lost six, three brothers and three sisters. And more, seventeen nieces and nephews. To be telling the story every day here, it's a big sacrifice! But we do it because we don't want it to be forgotten. And we need to maintain the place, so we. . . . This is our work . . . if you give here, it goes for the garden. It helps us a lot. This isn't just for our personal use. And, and we do have some things here that were made in the community, for you to buy.

Father Dan quietly thanks her. He hesitates and then hands her the pile of English-language versions of Rufina's testimony he has with him. He does not buy anything.

*   *   *

Father Dan's encounter with Raquel, and then with the women in the gift shop, could be interpreted in many different ways. He wields an intense desire to connect, not only through the medium of Shannon's and Ellen's translations but through his searching eye contact, his deeply inclined posture. By now, he feels that he is part of the story, whether as a complicit North American who has continually protested his government's actions and asked for forgiveness from the victims or as a longtime solidarity activist who has returned again and again to bring spiritual and material support. Raquel at first welcomes his involvement in her narration, at his encouragement shyly describing her own place in the story. Indeed, as she is a Márquez Chicas, her family has been at the center of the events, even if she had not yet been born when the massacre happened. But Father Dan's yearning to participate, to take part in the telling of El Mozote, eventually makes her uneasy. How can she interrupt a tall (if bent with age) white foreigner? She grows quieter as he continues. She tries to return to the story that she has been telling to tourists for six years, listing facts and incidents, pointing to places. Returning to review these interactions sometimes makes us (Ellen and Leigh) uncomfortable, too. Father Dan's interventions could be construed as colonizing invasions—or perhaps just hapless discursive embraces. We are too familiar with this kind of ethical ruminating, this anthropological anxiety about interrupting others' stories with our own words, whether theoretical or literary.

The tour is supposed to end at the gift shop—where, perhaps safely shielded from the sacred grounds of the church and memorial site, money can change hands. To Father Dan, however, the exchange of currency is beside the point (though he has joined the other delegation members in donating after Raquel's tour). Perhaps like returning anthropologists with their digital recorders and research assistants, he hungrily continues efforts to exchange feelings, asking for more stories, more experience, more affect. The woman behind the counter abruptly pulls out her numbers as if reading from her identification card—the six siblings, the seventeen nieces and nephews. But she also reminds him how much pain, how much emotion work, has gone into the production of this commodity of suffering, and how much labor is condensed, invisibly, into such public sharing with strangers: "It isn't easy. . . . This is our work." The money "isn't just for our personal use," she stresses, recognizing, perhaps, how the testimonies offered at the El Mozote site combine an aura of sacred pilgrimage with what some might see as a profane vacation distraction.

Her impatience is palpable. She monetizes her authenticity, asking for cash after she lists her own statistics of loss. The numbers are shocking. *And yet they are not enough.* Tourists, and anthropologists, want more. Father Dan, almost like an anthropologist returning to a field site with an academic monograph, awkwardly offers a photocopied English-language version of Rufina's testimony that he has been carrying for the delegation.

What does all of this have to do with that image of the baby pierced by a bayonet? Eight-month-old Isabel Claros Amaya, Rufina's daughter, did die that December 11, 1981, torn from her mother's breast, murdered and then burned into a charred black corpse along with her brother Cristino, her sisters Lolita and Lilian, and her father, Domingo Claros, who was almost blind (Henríquez Consalvi 2010, 84). Raquel follows this story line—the script, if you will—for the tourists rather than describing events from her own family's perspective, as Father Dan had apparently hoped. She inevitably omits many details. She also does not repeat something that Rufina always said, that some soldiers recoiled at killing children but were ordered to do so. Memory, of course, is always unstable, whether it is repeated endlessly for tourists or stored away in sacred scrolls. Does it matter whether *the way* Salvadoran soldiers ended Isabel's short life is precisely rendered? Does it matter that many visitors to El Mozote leave with vivid images of an impaled infant, or of children's bodies hanging from trees—the latter, at least, an empirically false image?

Like so many travelers to the Global South in a quest for connection, Father Dan wants an authentic trace of history. He seeks both the universality of human experience and the radical otherness of peasant revolution. In El Mozote the members of the women's collective who repeat these stories undoubtedly hope to honor the memory of the dead. But they also need to survive. Most if not all of them are single mothers with limited possibilities. Their stories of suffering seem to be all that they have to trade. Indeed, stories of suffering are what the tourists want. Ultimately the desires of the locals and the tourists differ, and are even conflicting. Perhaps tourists want a brush with radical alterity, a taste of authentic suffering, and/or a distraction from their own troubles. Maybe the tour guides want to feed their children and/or to honor their relatives who died. But somehow they meet and mingle uneasily in the plaza at the center of El Mozote. There, in northern Morazán in El Salvador, as in many sites of tragedy, a marketplace has emerged in which tour guides truck in stories of suffering.

"When suffering is reified into the apparent solidity of death," Ellen has written, "rather than stiffly bowing out of the circulation of values, out of meanings that make up culture, it becomes particularly prone to exchange, its (pseudo)commodity phase immanent. Death becomes the moment of exchange that makes possible a new, potentially agentive, value. It transforms a body considered somewhat autonomous in Western metaphysics into a sign exchanged for meaning among the living" (Moodie 2006, 68–69). More than thirty years ago, the dead bodies of the victims of El Mozote briefly became valued as news items and evidence of human-rights violations (for which the United States would place a few conditions on the money sent to the Salvadoran government). They became valued as objects of study by journalists and social scientists, including both co-authors of this article; they became symbols of impunity, proof of ongoing injustice.

That particular export economy of pain, vetted by Americas Watch and Amnesty International, was supposed to bring peace to El Salvador. But what it brought was (market) freedom under the cover of a (pseudo)democracy forced onto oligarchic structures (Robinson 2003). In an environment in which market thinking pervades social life, and in a context of bleak economic prospects in a marginal rural department of a poor country, perhaps it only makes sense that some (but not all) tour guides would try to hype the value of their product, that they would invent and repeat tales of horror, that they would produce increasingly fantastic stories of babies tossed into the air to hurtle down onto waiting blades. One might ask, Do the guides who embellish get more donations than others? Does this "inflation" devalue the bodies and ultimately the very history that has produced this place as a dark tourist attraction? Should we as anthropologists debunk these practices in the name of science or integrity or simple accuracy? But if we do so (and we may be doing so right now), could we also be supporting other kinds of troubling beliefs, echoing, in some sense, those who denied the totality of Rigoberta Menchú's account when an anthropologist questioned parts of her story?

We could end this chapter on this note of dissonance. Perhaps it really does not matter so much that the travelers and the tour guides—or endlessly returning anthropologists and their confidants/consultants/friends, for that matter—do not quite get each other, that their interactions are friction-filled misunderstandings. But the story does not end here.

* * *

We end this story with Esmeralda, a young woman of El Mozote. Just twenty, she is an FMLN activist and devout Catholic who attends mass with Father Rogelio Ponceele in Perquín. She was born the year the war ended, in 1992. By then members of her family had returned to Morazán from refugee camps in Honduras. They settled about an hour south of El Mozote. They finally made it back home in 1999, when Esmeralda was seven.

In a 2011 interview with Tara McGovern, a student member of the research team, Esmeralda laughs as she talks about her dreams of learning English and becoming a tour guide. As they sit at the kitchen table, shooing away chickens, she explains how as a child she had been fascinated by the buses full of people who came to hear about the history of the place—of her home. She would listen to older people talk about what happened. Her mother had told her how the refugee camp's popular education and conscientization processes had opened space for survivors to explore their past trauma and to claim their history.[22]

"The war left many histories," Esmeralda explains. "All these foreigners have read these books, and reports, and they want to know more. So they have the opportunity to travel, to come to the country. They want to know the history of our country! They come here to find out. So we have to explain it to them."

Tara suggests that Esmeralda must already have a lot of practice telling people about El Mozote. But Esmeralda does not feel that she is ready to do so yet: "I don't know anything. I just know what people told me." She assures Tara that now she has read a book, though. She names *Luciernagas en El Mozote*, the volume that includes Rufina Amaya's testimony, as if to bolster the credibility of her account.

She is not (yet) a tour guide. Perhaps for that reason, her story is not rote: it combines her mother's account with the dominant narrative of events. Like Raquel Márquez's family, Esmeralda's family had left El Mozote before the massacre took place. Her grandmother and mother fled two days before the soldiers arrived. Like many people, they had heard rumors that something was going to happen, that the army was coming. So they hightailed it into the mountains, walking all day and all night. Her mother was just nine, but she has described to Esmeralda how she vividly remembers the view from a mountain looking down toward El Mozote—and seeing smoke rising into the sky.

"They killed the people," Esmeralda explains. "They killed everyone. They gathered up the children, the adults, they took young girls into the hills and raped them, and then they burned them, and from far away you could see the smoke. The smoke, nothing more." Her sister's father-in-law would later tell the family about how he went to see El Mozote shortly after the massacre. All he saw were piles of bodies, "totally black."

Esmeralda is proud, she says, to be from such a historical place. Her pride seems to arise in part from the recognition offered by the outsiders, who have read so much and who look to people like her to know more. It is the massacre, the tragedy, their pain, that now gives them value in this economy, she seems to be saying—and in many ways like the woman in the gift shop, she is acknowledging that the story of their anguish is their ticket to survival. Esmeralda is young; right now she is excited about sharing this story. She repeats over and over how it is so *bonito*, so nice, to tell people their history.

Esmeralda represents a new generation of Salvadorans, seeking both survival and social transformation, like her parents and grandparents who organized and worked in the 1970s and 1980s (as did generations before, as well). Like them, she draws on the congealed labor of her forebears, in the form of their war-era suffering. But she does not only see this labor as something to be exchanged for money. She sees it as part of her heritage, something that she, along with young anthropology students like Tara, needs to share with others, with people like Father Dan and John from Sacred Heart, as well as with her fellow Salvadorans. If that is so, it may be that this (undeniable) commodification of history and the (inevitable) growth of tourism do not have to mean forgetting or erasure but rather a renewal: keeping alive a tradition of passing on the stories of parents and grandparents, not just to their children but to the rest of the world—if it comes to listen.

Notes

1.   This material is largely based on work supported by the National Science Foundation under Grant No. BCS-0962643 from the Cultural Anthropology Program as well as a grant from the University of Illinois Research Board. Any opinions, findings, and conclusions or recommendations expressed in this material are those

of the authors and do not necessarily reflect the views of the National Science Foundation.

2.   The names of the church in Illinois, its members, and its sister community in El Salvador have been changed for this chapter.

3.   Raquel refers to Rufina Amaya as she is commonly known, the "only survivor" in the sense that she was someone who was caught up in the massacre, apprehended by the army, and somehow escaped. In fact, a few others are also believed to have survived similarly to Rufina. Raquel also uses the word *survivor* for people from the community who left the immediate area before the massacre.

4.   This image has become iconic of the El Mozote massacre and appears on T-shirts and artisan products sold in northern Morazán and elsewhere in the country.

5.   El Mozote and the surrounding region were home to many landless and land-poor people who worked seasonally on large estates harvesting coffee and other export crops, mainly during the November to January period. Other people had gone into the mountains near the Honduran border to cut timber and saw it into planks.

6.   A July 2012 estimate of victims of the massacre compiled by a team working with El Mozote's Pro-Human Rights Association, composed of survivors and family members of the victims, was 1,061 dead, adjusted to 988 in June 2019.

7.   See Danner 1994, 72–74; Amaya, Danner, and Henríquez Consalvi 1996, 16; Henríquez Consalvi 2010, 84.

8.   The story of the impaled child may not be apocryphal, but neither was it a common feature of the massacre. Mark Danner (1994, 76–77, 79) offers an anonymous account of an Atlacatl officer who responded to one soldier's reticence to kill children by throwing a small boy into the air and impaling him in the manner described by the guides; he also cites Chepe Mozote, age ten at the time of the massacre, who said that he saw children being hanged and one three-year-old being tossed into the air to be stabbed with a bayonet. The impaling also found a place in the Tutela Legal report (2008, 58). Danner is clear, however, that this event (if it occurred) did not take place around the church and that Rufina Amaya was not positioned to see the children. Leigh Binford ([1996] 2016, 320n10) writes in a revised and expanded version of his monograph on El Mozote that the point is less that this and other horrendous incidents did not occur "but that such macabre images are those most likely to be engraved in visitors' minds and repeated to others when they return to their places of origin. The callousness required to carry out such acts takes precedence over routinized executions in which people were lined up and gunned down in open fields after being forcefully herded into some edifice."

9.   Northern Morazanians are very aware that U.S. visitors can, after paying airfare and taking four- or five-hour flights, enter El Salvador easily. A ninety-day tourist visa, issued in the international airport in Comalapa, costs ten dollars. Unless wealthy or otherwise connected, most Salvadorans wishing to go to the United States embark on a risky journey across three countries led by coyotes (people smugglers) who charge upward of six thousand dollars per person.

10. A year and a half later, in Guayaquil, Ecuador, the court would find the Salvadoran state guilty of these charges. An amnesty law passed in 1993 (overturned in 2016) had prevented the military officers involved from being tried in El Salvador. But the court ruling requires the Salvadoran government to investigate the massacre and to exhume, identify, and return remains of victims to their families. The tribunal also ordered economic reparations, a health program for the communities in which the massacre victims lived, and a military human-rights education program. See Corte Interamericana de Derechos Humanos (CIDH), Caso Masacres de El Mozote y lugares aledaños vs. El Salvador, Sentencia de 25 de octubre de 2012; Binford (1996) 2016. A year after the overturning of the amnesty law, eighteen former, high-ranking military officials, including retired general José Guillermo García Merino, now eighty-four years old, were put on trial for the massacre by a provincial judge. These proceedings are ongoing, running into 2019.

11. Whereas this observation may (or may seem to) be the case, tourism is a poor substitute for progressive social transformation, as a close reading of Babb's work makes clear.

12. Danner (1994) would report that many people in El Mozote were evangelical Christians, an assertion that Binford ([1996] 2016) disputed.

13. Contrast Danner 1994, 89, with Amaya, Danner, and Henríquez Consalvi 1996, 19.

14. The press provided substantial coverage of the massacre until the Reagan administration published the results of an "investigation" that disputed the Bonner and Guillermoprieto accounts. Between January 1983 and December 1989, major U.S. and Canadian newspapers cited El Mozote in a mere fifteen articles. See Binford (1996) 2016, 3–4.

15. For more on the Catholic Worker movement, see the organization's website at http://www.catholicworker.org/.

16. By grouping these visitors, we do not mean to suggest that the experiences they seek are all the same, or even very similar. Different motivations have very different implications for present and future relationships.

17. For more on this pairing, see the sister cities' website at https://www.elsalvador solidarity.org/Committees/cambridge-san-jose-las-flores-sister-city-project/.

18. "Expensive" meaning twenty-five U.S. dollars per night.

19. In 2011 locals were worried for the delegation's safety after the murders there of a health promoter and her son. For most of this trip, Sacred Heart visitors traveled back to a hostel, more than an hour away, each night. With the increasingly dangerous conditions in El Salvador, and Father Dan's ill health, the Sacred Heart-La Cruz relationship has not continued.

20. For this newspaper article, see Rohter 1996.

21. Although Ellen's field notes do not elaborate on Father Dan's reference, it is possible that he was speaking about the human-rights certifications required in the early 1980s in order to continue military assistance. The first one was on January 28, 1982. After four certifications, President Ronald Reagan let the bill lapse via pocket

veto. Congressman O'Neill did continue to fight for conditions on military aid to El Salvador. See Shapiro and Reid 1984.

22. Recall Raquel Márquez's telling the tourists that it was in Honduras that Rufina Amaya inspired people in the community to examine the events. See also Todd 2010, 165–89.

References

Amaya, Rufina, Mark Danner, and Carlos Henríquez Consalvi. 1996. *Luciernagas en El Mozote*. San Salvador: Ediciones Museo de la Palabra.

Arias, Arturo, ed. 2001. *The Rigoberta Menchú Controversy*. Minneapolis: University of Minnesota Press.

Babb, Florence E. 2011. *The Tourism Encounter: Fashioning Latin American Nations and Histories*. Stanford, Calif.: Stanford University Press.

Binford, Leigh. (1996) 2016. *The El Mozote Massacre: Human Rights and Global Implications*. Revised and expanded edition (original title: *The El Mozote Massacre: Anthropology and Human Rights*). Tucson: University of Arizona Press.

Brenneman, Ron. 2013. *Perquín Musings: A Gringo's Journey in El Salvador*. Self-published.

Coutin, Susan Bibler. 1993. *The Culture of Protest: Religious Activism and the U.S. Sanctuary Movement*. Boulder, Colo.: Westview Press.

Danner, Mark. 1994. *The Massacre at El Mozote: A Parable of the Cold War*. New York: Vintage.

Henríquez Consalvi, Carlos. 1992. *La Terquedad del Izote: La historia de Radio Venceremos*. Mexico City: Diana.

Henríquez Consalvi, Carlos. 2010. *Broadcasting the Civil War in El Salvador*. Austin: University of Texas Press.

Hochschild, Arlie Russel. 1979. "Emotion Work, Feeling Rules, and Social Structure." *American Journal of Sociology* 85 (3): 551–75.

Howell, Brian. 2009. "Mission to Nowhere: Putting Short-Term Missions into Context." *International Bulletin of Missionary Research* 33 (4): 206–11.

Huyssen, Andreas. 2003. *Present Pasts: Urban Palimpsests and the Politics of Memory*. Stanford, Calif.: Stanford University Press.

Lennon, John, and Malcolm Foley. 2000. *Dark Tourism: The Attraction of Death and Disaster*. Stamford, Conn.: Cengage Learning.

MacCannell, Dean. 1999. *The Tourist: A New Theory of the Leisure Class*. 3rd ed. Berkeley: University of California Press.

McAlister, Melani. 2008. "What Is Your Heart For? Affect and Internationalism in the Evangelical Public Sphere." *American Literary History* 20 (4): 870–95.

Menchú, Rigoberta, and Elisabeth Burgos-Debray. 1987. *I, Rigoberta Menchú: An Indian Woman in Guatemala*. Translated by Ann Wright. New York: Verso.

Moodie, Ellen. 2006. "Microbus Crashes and Coca-Cola Cash: The Value of Death in 'Free Market' El Salvador." *American Ethnologist* 33 (1): 63–80.

Robinson, William. 2003. *Transnational Conflicts: Central America, Social Change, and Globalization*. New York: Verso Books.

Rohter, Larry. 1996. "El Mozote Journal: Where Countless Died in '81, Horror Lives On in Salvador." *New York Times*, February 12, 1996.

Shapiro, Margaret, and T. R. Reid. 1984. "Reagan Wins Narrowly on Aid to El Salvador." *Washington Post*, May 11, 1984.

Stoll, David. 1999. *Rigoberta Menchú and the Story of All Poor Guatemalans*. Boulder, Colo.: Westview Press.

Todd, Molly. 2010. *Beyond Displacement: Campesinos, Refugees, and Collective Action in the Salvadoran Civil War*. Madison: University of Wisconsin Press.

Trouillot, Michel-Rolph. 1995. *Silencing the Past: Power and the Production of History*. Boston: Beacon Press.

Tutela Lega del Arzobispado de San Salvador. 2008. *El Mozote: Lucha por la verdad y la justicia: Masacre a la inocencia*. San Salvador: Oficinas del Arzobispado de San Salvador.

SEVEN

Strangely, Touristically Familiar

Rio for a Carioca's Eyes

FERNANDO DE SOUSA ROCHA

> *Think of the long trip home.*
> *Should we have stayed at home and thought of here?*
> *Where should we be today?*
> *Is it right to be watching strangers in a play*
> *in this strangest of theatres?*
> —ELIZABETH BISHOP, "QUESTIONS OF TRAVEL"

One is never a tourist at home. One becomes a tourist when the suitcases are packed, hotel rooms reserved, arrangements made for transportation, and, last but not least, itinerary plans made, perhaps according to a guide that is easily found in any bookstore or online. But is it necessarily so? Does the maxim defining tourism still hold true if one expands the geographic scope of touristic sites to include one's own hometown? Such an expansion seems to be quite appropriate in the case of big cities, such as Rio de Janeiro. After all, aren't there areas or neighborhoods in our hometowns that we have never visited because the socioeconomic paths trodden in our lives did not take us there? And haven't we all, at least one day in our lives, gotten lost in our own hometowns? Haven't we all suddenly found ourselves in places that we have never seen, discovering a sense of being displaced in what should be a familiar geography, sometimes even to the point of feeling in danger? Existing close to residential and business areas and often unvisited by locals, touristic sites and traps only evince the uncanny ambiguity between familiarity and unfamiliarity that constitutes our lived experiences of hometowns. What I seek to explore in this article is precisely the experience of the familiar becoming uncannily, touristically foreign for a Carioca (a native of Rio de Janeiro) who strolls around and sees Rio's diverse locations, in which cultural, historical, natural, and touristic landscapes conflate. Beyond the unhomeliness of tourism, what one may experience as "home" may be traversed precisely by the inattentive but innovative inhabitation of the tourist. One is never more at home than as a tourist; one never achieves a higher sense of the familiar than as a foreigner.

Such a process of becoming strangers to ourselves—to use Julia Kristeva's (1991) expression—as our hometown becomes our own, particular touristic site calls for a fragmented discourse. I can only speak to the uncanny, touristic dislocation of native residents (both those originating from and those currently residing in a place) by using a discontinuous discourse through which I attempt to reenact (and not only represent) the touristic displacement experienced in our home geography.[1] Defamiliarization may be one of our most important practices in the present-day, globalized, neoliberal world, given that, as Richard Sennett (2005, 109, 117) notes, "the practice of modern democracy demands that citizens learn how to enter into the experience and interests of unfamiliar lives," not because we need to defend difference but rather because "alterity is missing." And yet, he continues, alterity constitutes the "social condition that holds out the promise of subjective freedom, freedom from arbitrary definition and identification" (113). It is thus fundamental, as Kristeva proposes, that we should be able to invite the foreigner to inhabit us; that we recognize that the foreigner has always already been there, in that place we have assigned to the self, the same, the homogeneous. "By recognizing him [the foreigner] within ourselves," Kristeva (1991, 1) reminds us, "we are spared detesting him in himself." Without that recognition, there can be no responsibility for the other, which is the ethical relationship that can guarantee the possibility of the human, as Levinas (1998) has taught us.[2]

My reenactment of touristic displacement resembles what Roland Barthes (2010, 3) calls his *dramatic method* as he reconstructs an amorous discourse, inasmuch as what matters is not a single, symptomatic subjectivity but rather the mise-en-scène of an utterance. What is thereby elicited is not a psychological portrait, for the contours of the self are of no importance; Barthes seeks, on the contrary, a structural portrait in which a place for speech emerges.[3] Such a nonsubjective place calls for a displacement and entails a taking root—as Barthes himself does when he has recourse to the original meaning of *discursus*—which, contradictorily, puts into play an uprooting of a being-in-place that fosters self-conceptions. Displacement as *dis-cursus* means that one must be "running here and there," occupied in "comings and goings" and in different "measures taken" (Barthes 2010, 3). Because such a discourse is articulated by means of displacement, the speaker/agent must resort to figures—for which Barthes refers back to the Greek meaning. A *scheme* (σχῆμα in Greek) thus emerges as a much livelier fashion of situating oneself in discourse, for it implies "the body's gesture caught in action" (Barthes 2010, 4). To exercise subjectivity within a discourse is, in this sense, a corporeal performance.

Schemes, in the Barthesian sense, are central to most touristic experiences nowadays. Tourists browse brochures, glance at pictures of unbelievably blue waters or well-known sites, check schedules and itineraries, and so forth. Tourism, for the most part, requires outlined drafts, plans, and designs that anticipate and organize a programmed performance whereby a specific taking-place is fostered. *Join us and you will be there*—touristic discourse appeals to contemporary subjectivities—*walking on those streets made famous in songs such as "The Girl from Ipanema," standing next to the world-renowned monument of Christ the Redeemer, lying in the tropical sun and enjoying a typical caipirinha.* Touristic schemes are a contractual statement that says that the tourist will be physically engaged in those narrated, photographed, and reconstructed spaces and cultural environments; they are a preoccupation to which postcards and posed (but also composed) pictures testify.

Schematic discourse, in the case of tourism, thus implies a taking-place, in the double sense of the expression: tourist-speakers must be situated geographically, while figures, as Barthes (2010, 5) notes, must retain a place within the discourse, "the figure must be there, the site (the compartment) must be reserved for it." That does not mean, however, that there should be a specific ordering of figures, a preordained sequence. On the contrary, "no logic links the figures, determines their contiguity" (Barthes, 2010, 6–7). No wonder touristic discourse should comprise postcards and posed (but also composed) photographs, for these items reflect the very fragmentation that cities represent to their inhabitants. From such fragments, differing narratives may be weaved. As Jonathan R. Wynn (2010, 150) points out, social actors such as tour guides "take everyday fragments, perhaps even the ephemera that have been left to the dustbins of history, and transform them into something new and, importantly, how these actions shape interactions in public space." What I would like to underscore here is the productive side of consumption, which, as Michel de Certeau (1998, xix) propounds, may be tactically employed. For de Certeau, a tactic "cannot count on a 'proper' (a spatial or institutional localization), nor thus on a borderline distinguishing the other as a visible totality." Instead, "a tactic insinuates itself into the other's place, fragmentarily, without taking it over in its entirety, without being able to keep it at a distance." While engaging with ways of poaching well-established narratives, constitutive of the familiar, my recounting does not aim at what Wynn (2012,337) describes as "manipulat[ing] unruly and ever-changing elements of the city into a coherent narrative," ultimately "creat[ing] a 'story arc' or metanarrative that keeps their stories threaded together" (Wynn 2010, 149). On the contrary, my narrative is an investment in snapshots—figures or topoi—to which the tourist-speaker has recourse without any order except for that of memory and volatile desires, "the ruses of other interests and desires that are neither determined nor captured by the systems in which they develop," as de Certeau (1998, xviii) points out. I would otherwise risk turning otherness into a thing, solidifying it, when I should be "sketching out its perpetual motion through some of its variegated aspects spread out before our eyes" (Kristeva 1991, 3). The discourse that I construct, therefore, consists of figures, touristic topoi that cannot be dissociated from the places that invite such a discourse. Unlike Barthes, however, I have let both memory and desire, so important for touristic discourse, dictate the ordering of the named figures.

Fortresses

In June 2012, Rio de Janeiro became once more the site for an international summit on sustainable development. The event's name, Rio+20, alluded to the twenty years that had passed from the first Earth Summit, which took place in 1992. As part of the events that ran parallel to meetings for heads of states—the meetings that really mattered and that didn't after all—the Instituto do Patrimônio Histórico e Artístico Nacional (IPHAN) organized a series of sightseeing tours.[4] A friend and I took part in two: one to the Forte de São José, a fort built in 1578 at the entrance to the Guanabara Bay, and the other to the Sítio Burle Marx, residence to the most famous Brazilian landscaper, Roberto Burle Marx.

The Forte de São José, which is part of the Fortaleza de São João, is located on the tip of a peninsula, in the present-day neighborhood of Urca.[5] At the other side of the entrance to the Guanabara Bay, on another rocky shore, is the Fortaleza de Santa Cruz. Both fortresses were built by the Portuguese (and later maintained by Brazilians) in order to protect the land from invaders and, as with their forts on the African and Indian shores, to safeguard their commercial interests in the area, interests that were here based on the discovery of brazilwood. In fact, the Portuguese were not the only Europeans economically attracted by the exploitation of brazilwood and its red dye. In 1555, the French founded on the bay an incipient colony, called France Antarctique, which the Portuguese dismantled by taking over the French Fort Colïgny (Nowell 1949). Three centuries later, as a direct consequence of the Christie Affair (when the British Royal Navy blocked Rio de Janeiro's port and captured five Brazilian ships), Emperor Dom Pedro II approved a renovation of the São José fort in order to better protect the city, then the capital of the empire.[6]

As a result of Rio de Janeiro's sprawling inland, the city has long outgrown the fort's capacity to protect it. The city can no longer be erased from the map (or at least one would hope), nor is violence descried on the horizon, on the masts of ships. Violence is not foreign to the city; on the contrary, it is inbred, part of the very structuring of the city. A tour of the fort is therefore not solely a journey back in history, to the years of the city's uncertain foundation. Perhaps most importantly, it represents a stepping outside of Rio. Unable to protect the city it helped to birth, the fort now protects tourists from the city they should be visiting. As a form of compensation, however, the fort grants its visitors

FIGURE 7.1 Inside the walls of the Forte de São José. Author's photograph.

unexpected views. For those who know Rio de Janeiro well and are accustomed to Sugarloaf Mountain's iconic presence in the cityscape, to see it from a different angle is indeed a marvel, a sight for Cariocas' eyes. In fact, most tourists who visit the fort seem to be residents of the city, perhaps Cariocas. Still part of the commercial flux of capital—it is, after all, a touristic site—the fort welcomes foreigners rather than barring them from the city. Yet it also appears to indicate that many of the city's hidden gems remain hidden—and justly so. Such a contradiction perhaps explains why the breathtaking, unique view of the Sugarloaf should match so perfectly with the fort's immensely thick walls and the narrow views that we get as we stand behind them. A foreign regard is kept at bay, precisely where the city began and has always ended: where its interior waters are dispersed into transoceanic ones. There, where everything is withheld and lost, we gain a Carioca viewpoint.

Unknowing, Forgetfulness

"Which place was this? What was it called?" Perhaps these are, nowadays, less common questions, unknown to young tourists and photographers. In the old days, when we had to wait a few days to finish taking all twenty-four or thirty-six pictures in a roll (provided one was not a compulsive photographer, which most people were not, given the price one had to pay for each roll) and perhaps a few more days for the pictures to be developed, we would often forget names: those of the places we visited, of the statues or plants we saw, of those little details in a church, which are specific and weird, and which no one but a specialist can remember. Now technology affords us the luxury of taking four hundred pictures in one afternoon and, back home, downloading all four hundred pictures to the computer. Taking pictures and downloading them on the same day, we are less prone to forget; yet can't we say that the same guiding notions of unknowing and forgetfulness still infiltrate our experiences of touristic sightseeing in the twenty-first century? Doesn't the exaggeratedly excessive number of pictures that we take nowadays, which should replace the lost memory, still function as a form of loss? Isn't excessiveness an unfruitful compensation, or affirmation, against forgetfulness, of an unnamable place, object, or experience?

   Due to excessiveness, the picture-perfect shot no longer appears to be a concern of ours. *It will come*—we seem to think. Just keep on pressing the shutter button, take as many pictures as you possibly can, and amid the ten or twelve pictures of the same scene (or building, plant, animal, etc.), one of those should be close to picture perfect. Although there is still hope in the tourist-photographers' eyes (hope for the picture-perfect shot), somehow our unconcern has altered our relationship to photographing and to the hope that goes with it. No wonder that postcards have become a thing of the past—not yet completely reduced to the overvalued thingness of antiquities but no longer an item that properly pertains to touristic experience. We post our photos in Facebook (or send them by email or use any other photo-sharing program), but we do not mail postcards. This change is not only a matter of timing (that is, because a postcard is "snail mail," as we so aptly call it) but, most importantly, one of focus: our interest does not lie anymore in sharing photographic depictions of touristic attractions, at least not when they stand by themselves.

When traveling was not as common an experience as it is nowadays, illustrated lectures were the best way to "travel" to distant lands.[7] These lectures consisted of glass slides with pictures of historic or exotic places, accompanied by descriptive readings. As a rule, the photographer or those traveling with him were not to appear in the picture, unless there was a purpose for their being in it.[8] What mattered, above all, was capturing a photographic representation of the place to make it present to the viewers as well as to make these viewers feel present in such a place, rather than to show them the meaning of "I've been there" that any photograph conveys once a traveler is in it. Compared thus to illustrated lectures, postcards represent a vulgarization of travel photography, inasmuch as personal notes substitute for the descriptive text of the former. A step further in this process of vulgarization is taken with personal photographs. For alongside the standard postcard picture of Christ the Redeemer, with writings on the back, there comes another picture (already classic now) of us standing in front of the Christ, with our arms stretched open, imitating the posture in the statue. What might be restricted with a postcard to the writing on its back, where we usually comment briefly about *our* experiences at those landmarks, switches entirely to the front. Photographs allow us to stamp our personal selves onto those landmarks. Yet such stamping also has its drawbacks. If, in illustrated lectures, photographs were used to enact public visual tours, now pictures have become part of our personal archives, functioning as mnemonic devices. The photograph turns out to be "a prop, a prompt, a pre-text: it sets the scene for recollection" (Kuhn 2003, 396). As such, the photograph may be of little to no interest to those who did not take it. What a bore, indeed, to have to sit through a show-off photographic session when relatives or friends want to share their touristic experiences—and "share" is, of course, a misnomer, a euphemism in the most optimistic perspective or a torture session in the worst-case scenario.

Can't Keep It in the Pants

Lapa is a bohemian district in Rio, recently revitalized with a number of bars and restaurants, which also host breathtaking musical performances, notably of samba and *chorinho*. Once a well-known zone of prostitution, Lapa has become, in the past few years, quite eclectic. On Friday and Saturday nights, with its main streets closed to traffic, the district is overcrowded with people who belong to the most disparate *tribos* (tribes)—from rappers and hip-hop dancers to LGBTQ+ folks to samba aficionados to, needless to say, tourists. Prostitutes are still seen, walking the streets and wearing skimpy clothes that might somehow attract new clients. Apparently, this invasive multitude, initially foreign to the area, did not scare away the prostitutes, whose silicone-filled butts and thick legs enter narrow buildings or run-down hotels, sometimes accompanied by men.

Such an agglomeration of people comes, as might be expected, at a price. Any bohemian district—take, for instance, Lisbon's Bairro Alto, which must be washed clean after a night's partying—faces serious problems concerning the disposal of trash and biological matter. City government therefore provides Rio's bohemians with portable restrooms, located near the Arcos da Lapa, the old aqueduct where the famous tram tracks now run. However, for bohemians and drunkards a walk to those portables might be an excruciating journey—or perhaps a nuisance. Who cares to walk down the street when conversation is so animated and—who knows?—you're finally hitting on that hottie or hunk next to you? For men, the solution is easily at hand: find a corner or stand against a wall or a car, unzip your pants, lower your briefs, and hold your dick out to finally take a piss. A habit of the past, as we see in an early nineteenth-century watercolor sketch made by French artist Jean-Baptiste Debret, public urination seems to have found, in crowds, its revival and surge, and not only in Lapa.[9] The same scene repeats itself at Pedra do Sal, a historic place due to its significance for Afro-Brazilian culture in Rio de Janeiro's downtown area. As one of the birthplaces of samba in the city, it remains an important place for listening to the music. However, when I visited the area for a performance, several men would at times stand in front of a wall and take a piss while enjoying the samba. Since the area is rather hilly, urine would invariably trickle down the sidewalks and streets, creating thin streams that one had to watch out for.

For "civilized" eyes, perhaps accustomed to Amsterdam's public urinals or to the ones that Rio de Janeiro's city government placed in the streets during the 2010 Carnival, the Carioca vogue might seem rather unhealthy, not to say completely unsanitary.[10] Yet one more aspect of public urination cannot be overlooked: it establishes an aggressively masculinized environment. The men claim a phallic, manly right over and appropriation of public spaces as these become dirtied with piss. By forcing others to step over and remain attentive to their piss streaks, which mix with beer, foul water, and spit, pissers turn streets and sidewalks into a phallic space. We traverse a masculinized territory, quite often with women's consent, if not altogether their encouragement. As I walked toward a busier street, where I could more easily catch a taxi, I saw a mother's nonchalance as she chatted with a friend, both laughing over a few glasses of beer. While she minded only her own business with her friend, her son, who seemed to be in his twos, peed at the leg of another white plastic table right next to them, trying to keep his balance and not to wet his own little crocs and watching his pee hit the pebbles and stream around them.

Inattention, Uninhabitation

Tourists and residents alike may find pleasure in walking through a city, whether one knows the city all too well or not at all.[11] While some people may feel inclined to pay attention to every detail, a Carioca who knows the city well may inattentively stroll down the streets. He is not there to see anything in particular, and so he may easily see nothing at all—that is, he refrains not from seeing but from registering anything that he sees. Each and every image is quickly erased, blurred in a forgetfulness that reflects on itself: one does not even remember that one should be remembering something—whatever that *thing* is—and thus the subject is released from oblivion. Forgetting no longer matters, but neither does remembering. For opposite reasons, tourists may also engage in this sort of inattentive spatial appropriation. Tourists have fixed objectives or destinations (e.g., "this morning we'll visit Rio's Jardim Botânico"), and thus the act of seeing—whether prior to departure, en route to a destination, or after the planned sightseeing—is always inattentive. Not yet or no longer at the place they intend(ed) to visit, tourists may disengage their eyes from whatever it is that they see and relieve themselves from the burdensome, narrow tasks of recording, storing, and remembering.[12]

Strangely enough, inobservant tourists (be them residents or foreigners) serve, while out and about, in the streets, to uninhabit space. If in the notion of inhabiting lies implicit a taking root whereby the void of space is filled with our presence, then to uninhabit is to undo such a process. To uninhabit is to dwell in displacement so as to induce a sense of pure spatiality, a detachment through which we prove to ourselves that the outside world stands alone, irrespective of ourselves. Tourism, in this sense, is a *pharmakon* for residence in a place and the habits that we form due to our repeated movement through familiarized spaces.[13] Yet the uninhabitation that tourism fosters also produces the proper place for (un)expected encounters. Freud (2003, 144) reveals as much in his essay in which he develops the notion of the uncanny (*unheimlich*) while recounting one of his sojourns in Italy. Seeing prostitutes at the windows of the houses, Freud is overtaken by the sensations of déjà vu and déjà vécu as he returns again and again to the same street. Freud's narrative lays bare the impossible but undeniable experience of the always already lived, which goes beyond personal memory. We are always anterior to ourselves, if for no other reason than that we are historical beings.

As I stand in front of the Centro Cultural Ação da Cidadania,[14] waiting for the bus to Burle Marx's *sítio*, my friend Maristela reveals to me that the construction site that I see across the street is actually an accidental finding of historical importance. In renovating Rio de Janeiro's port area with the ambitious

FIGURE 7.2 Excavations at the site of the Cais da Imperatriz and Cais do Valongo. Author's photograph.

FIGURE 7.3 Workers at the excavation site. Author's photograph.

project titled Porto Maravilha,[15] workers found under the cement the Cais da
Imperatriz, the wharf where Teresa Cristina, the princess of the Two Sicilies who
married Emperor Dom Pedro II by proxy, was welcomed into Brazilian life. The
same location is also, however, the site for the Cais do Valongo, where enslaved
Africans set foot in Rio de Janeiro for the first time. In 1843, in order to receive
Princess Teresa Cristina, the Cais do Valongo was renovated by French architect
Grandjean de Montigny and thus renamed Cais da Imperatriz (Porto Maravilha, n.d.). As I saw the past reemerge—and as it did so through the poorly paid
labor of African descendants (for the workers I saw were all Afro-Brazilians)—I
could no longer fend off the uncanny feeling that I was revisiting myself.

Pão de Açúcar and the Flamengo Gardens

Before subway stations opened in Copacabana and Ipanema, I had to take
the bus when going downtown. As the bus reached Botafogo, the view was
(and still is) breathtaking: the Sugarloaf would be on our right-hand side—
"standing majestically," I am inclined to say, but I refrain. I must stop myself in
my tracks, otherwise I would be lying. It is true: lying is also part of a touristic
memory. Looking at the pictures taken during a trip, who does not feel a sense

of extraordinariness? And yet we also disparage sightseeing spots that we cannot but see—for every good tourist visits them—given that they constitute precisely a "must see." Thus Itapuã Beach in Salvador is quite disappointing because it falls short of the cultural imaginary, as in Vinícius de Moraes and Toquinho's famous song "Tarde em Itapoã" (1971). The song speaks of an intense bodily pleasure based on a mixture of idleness, alcoholic lightheadedness, and the physicality of nature. Perhaps Moraes and Toquinho's Itapuã from the early 1970s has very little (or even nothing) to do with what we may presently experience there. And yet such disappointment seems to have less to do with the time gap and more to do with the discrepancies between reality and symbol.

I must therefore tell the truth: the Pão de Açúcar, as we Cariocas call Sugarloaf, is an endearing, quotidian sight, which the name given to the rock indicates. It is a sweet bread, to be savored daily—which I did and still do whenever I am in Rio—recalling Caetano Veloso's wonderful musical rendition of Oswald de Andrade's 1925 poem "Escapulário" (meaning a religious scapular). I hum and mentally sing the poem: "No Pão de Açúcar, de cada dia, dai-nos Senhor, a poesia de cada dia, no Pão de Açúcar . . . No Pão de Açúcar, de cada dia . . ." (In the Sugarloaf, of every day, give us oh Lord, our daily poetry, in the Sugarloaf . . . In the Sugarloaf, of every day . . .).[16] Andrade's concise, haiku-like poem easily lends itself to daily, devotional, prayerful repetitions, particularly when it becomes a samba, as in Veloso's song. Poem and music, together, invite us to a daily, impossible communion through bread and stone, poetry and touristic site. The Sugarloaf becomes, as Andrade proposes in his poems, a means of appropriating what is ours, even if that which we reclaim is—and Andrade pokes fun here at European travelers who visited Brazil—rather barbaric (see Andrade [1925] 2003).

But let us divert our eyes from the Sugarloaf and focus on our route, for the bus on its way downtown starts to curve to the right and then the left—regardless of whether one takes the Praia do Flamengo or Aterro route—and drives by landscaping art created by Burle Marx, the famous Brazilian landscape architect. To drive by is not the best way of appreciating Burle Marx's botanical compositions, but the drive is certainly greened by them. One never stops spotting new plants not previously noticed; one never tires of looking for the flowers that are in bloom. What catches my curiosity most, however, are not the trees and bushes but rather an exuberant flower and fruit (Amazonian-like to my eyes, which can only see exoticism in the jungle that is not bursting through my kitchen window) that grow on a tree found in the gardens of the Museum of Modern Art. *Abricó-de-macaco* is the name of the tree (in English, cannonball

FIGURE 7.4 The Sugarloaf, as seen from the Forte de São José. Author's photograph.

tree), and its fruit is of a perfect roundness, hanging from the trunk but so close that we have the impression that it grows on the trunk like distorted, monumental, brown jabuticabas (the fruit of Brazilian grapetrees). Its flower is no less impressive: red, fleshy petals, lip-like, and in its heart are white petals with rosy tentacles, mimicking a waterless sea anemone. After doing some research, I discovered that the tree is in fact native to the Amazon region, which suggests that not all touristic exoticism is off the mark.

Coité, Cuia

The Parque do Flamengo, with its countless trees and bushes, is Burle Marx's most visible and well-known botanical artwork. The lesser-known one is his *sítio*, a greenhouse and art studio situated in the westernmost part of the city, away from the hustle and bustle of the Zona Sul or the downtown area. His *sítio* is the quintessence of tropicalism: Burle Marx plays with the different shades of green in his arrangements and also with an array of sizes, shapes, and textures. As the tour group was strolling around the gardens, following in the guide's steps, my eyes caught sight of a *coité*, a green, round fruit, bigger than the size of a man's closed fist. Once it is dried up, the *coité* may be used to make a bowl, called in Portuguese *cuia*. Coincidentally, I had been listening to a CD with songs by Wilson Moreira and Nei Lopes (1980), two of the finest *sambistas* from Rio de Janeiro, in which one of the songs is titled precisely "Coité, cuia." The song is an ode to the *coité* and the *cuia* made from it, on the one hand alluding to the different Brazilian dishes that one may eat in it and the *cachaça* (a distilled spirit made from sugarcane juice) accompanying them, and on the other hand suggesting an overall know-how that links the techniques for making *cuias*, the taste for the dishes (and the *cachaça*), and the art of samba. As the singers put it, "Pra fazer cuia / também tem que ter ciência / Quem não tiver competência / Não vai ter bom paladar" (In order to make a *cuia* / One must also have science / Whoever does not have competence / Will not have good taste either). Science, competence, and taste (*ciência, competência, paladar*) are thus interconnected in fostering a broad mode of cognition of the Carioca sociocultural world.

Seeing a *coité* at Burle Marx's *sítio* is thus no trivial event: it speaks of an uncanny conjunction of practices, for Burle Marx's *sítio* is also nothing short of a techne that involves both an aestheticization of nature and an attunement to

FIGURE 7.5 *Coités* at the Sítio Burle Marx. Author's photograph.

the designs and technologies arising in nature. Lopes and Moreira invoke such a techne in their song when they state that a good *coité*, the real one, "tem que se cortar no mato"—that is, it must be cut right from the tree, in the woods. From the green forests to a person's hands, holding the food or the *cachaça*, while the person hears or plays samba, the *coité* (later turned into a *cuia*) exists on and partakes in a natural-social continuum. In a similar fashion, in Burle Marx's *sítio* visitors are exposed to a composition that integrates green gardens, architectural design, sculptures and paintings, salvaged stone and woodwork, tiles, tablecloths, and more. It is thus more than the synthesis of all the arts that Burle Marx admired in artists such as French architect Le Corbusier. If it is true that Burle Marx enjoyed citing Le Corbusier's idea that "one needs to surround oneself with objects of poetic emotion" (Eliovson 1991, 41), then the concept of art must be broadened to admit to its core all sorts of objects, as we see in Burle Marx's *sítio*. As a tropicalist, perverse mode of cognition, Burle Marx's *sítio* is a must-see—but only for those who have eyes to see, ears to hear, tongues to taste, and so forth.

Tourists to Ourselves

Our identities are anchored, in part, on a sense of belonging to a place. One is (or feels oneself to be) a Carioca, Chilango, Dubliner, Dakarois, or Azumaotoko because one was born in a place or because one has lived there long enough to identify with the place, that is, with its geography, its sociocultural life, and the narratives constituting it. I am a Carioca because many of the stories that I have to tell are set against Rio de Janeiro's streets, parks, and beaches; they involve its people. I am a Carioca because I have the urge to periodically return to Rio, as if in search of a feeling of homeness that can emerge only by displacement: a space that embraces me and at the same time rejects me. Such temporality, in its infinite returns to (de)familiarized homes that become the place for an encounter with the other, for a welcoming of the foreigner, might ultimately produce "something [more] like an older involvement than any rememberable deliberation constitutive of the human" (Levinas 1998, 114). At that time, when memory fails us, we face the other.

Alongside citizenship or homeness, what defines us today—if the world is truly globalized—is the constant possibility of not belonging, of being tourists.

To all those places that we do not call home or are not citizens of, we are, above all, tourists. Planned or haphazard, tourism is a mode of appropriating other places (and the foreignness residing in them), thereby displacing otherness. By means of tourism, in other words, otherness is partially uprooted; it no longer belongs here or there. Rather, it goes through a process of internalization, to the point that whatever was foreign, other, or strange to us is henceforth lodged within ourselves. Becoming tourists to ourselves is a manner of knowing—always fragmentarily, always incompletely—a tiny particle of such otherness, foreignness, or strangeness, but without quite doing so. We are, in the long run, always already tourists to ourselves, always facing the familiar strangeness (and the strange familiarity as well) of selfhood.

Notes

1. Coincidentally, in a three-volume history of the Urca neighborhood in Rio de Janeiro (Schmidt de Almeida 1998), the title chosen by the researchers involved in the historiographical project was precisely "Discourse Fragments." Although the authors do not explain their choice for the title, it implies the notion that history can be reconstructed only fragmentarily.

2. Between 2014, when I wrote the first version of this chapter, and today, November 2018, history happened. Brazilians have elected as president someone who seems to have a proclivity to authoritarianism. Defamiliarization and otherness have thus regained urgency, but they have also obtained new meanings. A familiar land-scape—my hometown, my home country—has turned somewhat unfamiliar, not because of practices that an *I* may engage in, as I attempt to do in this chapter, but because of an imposition by sociopolitical forces, achieved by means of a national election (that is, a legally sanctioned collective decision).

3. In the original text, Barthes (1977, 7) calls this structural portrait a "place de parole." Bearing in mind that Barthes borrows the term *parole* from Saussure, this place from whence one speaks constitutes the possibility of making use of a structured language (*langue*, for Saussure) through which a person constructs and situates himself or herself as a speaking subject.

4. IPHAN is a government institute that was founded in 1937 during Getúlio Var-gas's regime and is now part of the Ministry of Culture. Its objective is to preserve any cultural expression, material or immaterial (even geographic sites), that are particularly relevant for Brazil's cultural identity.

5. For a very succinct chronology of the Fortaleza de São João, see Barretto 1958, 229–37.

6. For a discussion of the Christie Affair, see Graham 1962; for Christie's own account, see Christie 1865; and for Brazilians' views on the affair and British influ-ence in the newly independent nation, see Forman 2000.

7. For a brief analysis of the careers of two of the most important American lecturers, see Barber 1993.
8. In Francis Frith's 1860 photograph of the Great Wall of China, for instance, the photographer had three of his companions stand and sit by the wall in order to visually depict its magnitude (Time-Life Books 1982, 47).
9. Debret was the history painter in the Missão Artística Francesa (French Artistic Mission), which arrived in Brazil in 1816. Under the auspices of King Dom João VI, the mission helped foster the fine arts in Brazil, which had housed the Portuguese court since 1808. In Debret's sketch, the offender is a white man of means. But today, since public urination is now limited to people with "no class," it may easily be seen as a backward act. See Bandeira and Lago 2008, 442.
10. For a photograph of the urinals in Rio, see Neno 2010.
11. For a point of comparison, see Rubem Fonseca's short story "The Art of Walking in the Streets of Rio de Janeiro," which follows streets and sanitation worker Augusto as he wanders the streets of Rio, attentively observing all that he comes across (Fonseca 2013).
12. If, as Walter Benjamin (1969, 240) observes, the distracted person also forms habits, then inattention stands, paradoxically, on the threshold between habitualness and fortuity.
13. I am using the term *pharmakon* with the double meaning that Jacques Derrida (1981, 70) assigns to it—that is, as both medicine and poison.
14. Ação da Cidadania, founded by sociologist Herbert "Betinho" de Souza in 1993, is an NGO whose objective is to eradicate hunger and misery from Brazil, for both are seen as being incompatible with democracy. The Centro Cultural Ação da Cidadania is located in Rio de Janeiro's first warehouse. Initially built in 1871, this structure was renovated in 2002 to house a center for excellence in cultural entrepreneurship and social inclusion.
15. Two stated objectives of this project are to improve living conditions of residents of the area near Rio de Janeiro's port as well as to redevelop the area in order to make it more culturally active and attractive. For a detailed description of the project, see Porto Maravilha's website, http://portomaravilha.com.br/summary.
16. Although its literal rendering would be "sweet bread" or "sugar bread," *pão de açúcar* (sugarloaf) actually means the conical form in which refined sugar was produced, transported, and commercialized. For the song, see Veloso 1975.

References

Andrade, Oswald de. (1925) 2003. "Escapulário." In *Pau Brasil*, 99. São Paulo: Globo.
Bandeira, Julio, and Pedro Corrêa do Lago. 2008. *Debret e o Brasil: Obra completa, 1816–1831*. Rio de Janeiro: Capivara.
Barber, Theodore. 1993. "The Roots of Travel Cinema: John L. Stoddard, E. Burton Holmes and the Nineteenth-Century Illustrated Travel Lecture." *Film History* 5:68–84.

Barretto, Annibal. 1958. *Fortificações do Brasil: Resumo Histórico*. Rio de Janeiro: Biblioteca do Exército Editora.

Barthes, Roland. 1977. *Fragments d'un Discours Amoureux*. Paris: Seuil.

Barthes, Roland. 2010. *A Lover's Discourse: Fragments*. Translated by Richard Howard. New York: Hill and Wang.

Benjamin, Walter. 1969. "The Work of Art in the Age of Mechanical Reproduction." In *Illuminations: Essays and Reflections*, translated by Harry Zohn, 217–51. New York: Schocken Books.

Christie, W. D. 1865. *Notes on Brazilian Questions*. London: MacMillan.

De Certeau, Michel. 1998. *The Practice of Everyday Life*. Translated by Steven Rendall. Berkeley: University of California Press.

Derrida, Jacques. 1981. "Plato's Pharmacy." In *Dissemination*, translated by Barbara Johnson, 61–171. Chicago: University of Chicago Press.

Eliovson, Sima. 1991. *The Gardens of Roberto Burle Marx*. Portland, Ore.: Saga Press.

Fonseca, Rubem. 2013. "The Art of Walking in the Streets of Rio de Janeiro." In *Winning the Game and Other Stories*, translated by Clifford E. Landers, 107–44. North Dartmouth, Mass.: Tagus Press.

Forman, Ross G. 2000. "Harbouring Discontent: British Imperialism Through Brazilian Eyes in the Christie Affair." In *An Age of Equipoise? Reassessing Mid-Victorian Britain*, edited by Martin Hewitt, 225–43. Aldershot, UK: Ashgate.

Freud, Sigmund. 2003. *The Uncanny*. Translated by David McLintock. London: Penguin.

Graham, Richard. 1962. "Os fundamentos da ruptura de relações diplomáticas entre o Brasil e a Grã-Bretanha em 1863: 'A Questão Christie.'" *Revista de História* 49:117–38.

Kristeva, Julia. 1991. *Strangers to Ourselves*. Translated by Leon S. Roudiez. New York: Columbia University Press.

Kuhn, Annette. 2003. "Remembrance: The Child I Never Was." In *The Photography Reader*, edited by Liz Wells, 395–401. London: Routledge.

Levinas, Emmanuel. 1998. *Entre Nous: On Thinking-of-the-Other*. Translated by Michael B. Smith and Barbara Harshay. New York: Columbia University Press.

Moreira, Wilson, and Nei Lopes. 1980. "Coité, Cuia." Track A2 on *A Arte Negra de Wilson Moreira e Nei Lopes*, Fênix 31C 034 421196, LP.

Neno, Mylène. 2010. "Banheiro químico aberto chama atenção durante desfile de bloco no Rio." G1, February 14, 2010, http://g1.globo.com/Carnaval2010/0,,MUL1490901 -17812,00-BANHEIRO+QUIMICO+ABERTO+CHAMA+ATENCAO +DURANTE+DESFILE+DE+BLOCO+NO+RIO.html.

Nowell, Charles E. 1949. "The French in Sixteenth-Century Brazil." *Americas* 5 (5): 381–93.

Porto Maravilha. n.d. "Historical and Archaeological Circuit Celebrating African Heritage." Accessed August 24, 2013, http://portomaravilha.com.br/historical_and _archeological.

Schmidt de Almeida, Roberto. 1998. *Fragmentos Discursivos de Bairros do Rio de Janeiro: Urca*. Vol. 3, *Mapas e Fotos*. Rio de Janeiro: UNI-RIO.

Sennett, Richard. 2005. "Capitalism and the City: Globalization, Flexibility, and Indifference." In *Cities of Europe: Changing Contexts, Local Arrangements, and the Challenge to Urban Cohesion*, edited by Yuri Kazepov, 109–22. London: Blackwell.

Time-Life Books. 1982. *Travel Photography*. Alexandria, Va.: Time-Life Books.

Veloso, Caetano. 1975. "Escapulário." Track 13 on *Jóia*, Philips 6349 132, LP.

Wynn, Jonathan R. 2010. "City Tour Guides: Urban Alchemists at Work." *City and Community* 9 (2): 145–64.

Wynn, Jonathan R. 2012. "Guides Through Cultural Work: A Methodological Framework for the Study of Cultural Intermediaries." *Cultural Sociology* 6 (3): 336–50.

PART III

Departures

EIGHT

Circles of Power Children of Resistance, Or My Rules of Engagement

GINA ATHENA ULYSSE

Sitting in the back of an air-conditioned tourist bus
snaking through the more presentable parts of old habana
I admit I have been an *enfant terrible*
a terrible terrible child
who unhappily absorbed rows of acid-rain-stained
colonial mansions with open jealousy windows
for protruding foreign eyes to stare
extended crossed legs reclined in hardbacked chairs facing
fifty's style tvs framed in wooden boxes with pointy legs
my foreign eyes protrude
desperate for a sense of the real cuba
not the folkloric performances
or well structured tours that
make a commodity of the revolution
and tied it to black insurrections of the past
while hiding away present-day black sufferrations

global apartheid
sister faye calls it
Shout out to the Comaroffs

why is it that everywhere we go in the world
darker skinned people are always at the bottom
always at the end of the line?

I have been an *enfant terrible*
a terrible terrible child
arrogantly impatient
with the same circles of power
that came even with socialism

I wanted to discover my cuba
get a sense of my cuba
not the guarded tours designed
to keep you away from the realities
silenced
because the revolution worked
          But it didn't fix everything
because the revolution worked
          But it didn't fix everything
because the revolution worked
          But it couldn't fix everything
          It could not fix everything
so now we pretend
that black blood flows through us
that we have black friends   blackness is cuba
that cuba is a black woman with a big behind
with a fat cigar hangin' in her mouth

I wanted to find my cuba
not be force-fed black performances
of blackness made for tourist consumption
I have been a terror
so quick to question without
even giving it a chance to be
so quick to question without

even giving it a chance to be
                                            what ever it is
                              whateva
I know I have seen it all before
I just came from haiti
it's the same thing wherever you go
black people at the bottom of the stairs
black people at the end of the line
black people in the back door
black people performing
recreating minstrelsy
five bucks for filming and picture taking please
blackness as commodity

              so what do you have to complain about now?
                                            she asked me

tired of my own repetitious tirades
about being force-fed blackness
performances of blackness
folklore devoid of spirit
made to satisfy the urge to find roots
made to satisfy the urge to find roots
                                   to claim roots where some exist
                                   to claim roots where some exist
roots to justify diasporic existences
why the hell are we consuming here
stereotypical images we'd boycott over there

my spirit wanted to cry
                     wail
                          scream
                                 holler

stop force feeding me blackness
stop force feeding me my blackness

stop fucking force feeding me my own blackness
I have been an *enfant terrible*
a terrible terrible child

    Are you actually planning on staying in academia

                                    she asked me

    there are rules you know
    you have to play by the rules
    until you can get to a point
    where you will have power
    and eventually make changes
    and make your own history

MAKE my own history
Make my OWN history
Make my own HISTORY

my history has already been made
do I have to name them
                retrace the lineage
              my lineage
               your lineage
                   Our lineage

the millions and millions of lives
            of pacifists
            of fighters
            of warriors
the lives of those
who committed suicide
who fought
who claimed freedom and made it theirs
who died
why do I have to start over
why do I have to start over
why do I have to start over
and recreate the wheel that they were tied to

and recreate the wheel that they had to go through
and recreate the training wheel   lab rats
wheels that keep going and going and going
and going and won't stop
until we say we won't get on the bus
because the road has been mapped
the road has been traveled before
the rails of this road had been forged
by the billions and billions of feet
footsteps of those who
bled and died
so we could stand here
so I can stand here
facing you
                    impatiently waiting
to hear you tell me when I can move
to hear you tell me when I can take
                              the step that won't offend
                              the step that won't threaten
                              you

when knives and daggers surround me
I don't fight
I get on my knees and I pray
I scream
when my Spirit is under siege
I don't fight
I holler while waiting for deliverance
waiting for deliverance
that won't come
for a deliverance
that can't come
because the wheel spins and spins and spins
only to keep spinning and won't stop
until we say we won't get on the bus
this is why I can't wait
no this is why I won't wait

too many have died for me to be here
too many have already died for me to stand here
waiting
            waiting
wondering when you will face me and finally admit
that this is not a duel
you didn't bring your weapons
hell! you've hidden your weapons
so we can't fight

so I have to decide
I have to decide
I have to recreate the wheel
if I get on this training wheel
my spirit will weaken
my spirit will weaken
in this cage that is yours
my spirit will weaken in this cage
that is your stage your fortress
your power your ivory tower
this is why I can't wait
this is why I must   rage
this is why I yell and will always holler
silence is suffocating me
and if I don't speak
and if I decide to play by the rules
will I know me
will I remember me
who I am and who I am supposed to be
pacifist?
fighter?
warrior
self-protector
who will guide me
who will lead me if I abandon my soul
I have been an *enfant terrible*
a terrible terrible child

When my spirit is under siege
I look to the future and feel weak
I look to the future and   feel weak
knowing that knives and daggers surround me
while I   wait   for history to absolve me
while I wait to make a history
knives and daggers surround me
waiting for me to make a move
waiting for me to try to whisper cricks
not cracks
cricks cracks
crick crack
krik
–krak
shrieks to fill silenced spaces
once full of loud voices
that   have been drowned by the circles of power
threatened by terrible children tied to their truths
terrible terrible children bound to their truths
unruly narrow-minded children
who need a long time

to accept that   they come from
long lines of
pacifists
fighters
warriors
who have already paid their dues
they have already paid my dues
so when I tell you I won't start here
because my ancestors have already been there
so when I tell you I won't start here
because my ancestors have already been there
know that I am on the offense
know that I have declared war
know that I shall win
since I am here for but one reason

I am here to face you
I am here to look you in the eye
and challenge you to duel
I am here to claim back my spirit
        while standing on the piles of dust
        made of the carcasses of my ancestors
to take it and let it be
let it roam the streets of this earth while looking above
searching for a higher self
because my dear enemy
my dear friend
after all   that   is really
all I was brought
down here to do

Contributors

Ruth Behar was born in Havana, Cuba, and grew up in New York. She is the Victor Haim Perera Collegiate Professor of Anthropology at the University of Michigan. A writer and a cultural anthropologist, she has lived and worked in Spain, Mexico, and Cuba. She is known for her humanistic approach to understanding identity, immigration, and the search for home in our global era. Her nonfiction books include *Traveling Heavy: A Memoir in between Journeys* (Duke University Press, 2013); *An Island Called Home: Returning to Jewish Cuba* (Rutgers University Press, 2007); and *Translated Woman: Crossing the Border with Esperanza's Story* (Beacon Press, 1993). She is also the author of a coming-of-age novel, *Lucky Broken Girl* (Nancy Paulsen Books, 2017), and a bilingual book of poems, *Everything I Kept/Todo lo que guardé* (Swan Isle Press, 2018).

Leigh Binford teaches in the Department of Sociology and Anthropology at the College of Staten Island of the City University of New York (CUNY) and is a member of the graduate faculty in the PhD Anthropology Program at the CUNY Graduate Center. He has carried out fieldwork in various areas of central and southern Mexico and in northern Morazán, El Salvador. In 2016, the University of Arizona Press published *The El Mozote Massacre: Human Rights and Global Implications*, an updated and revised edition of *The El Mozote Massacre: Anthropology and Human Rights*, first published in 1996. He recently completed a book-length manuscript, tentatively titled "Fabio's Story: Narrating Popular Intellectuals in the Salvadoran Revolution."

M. Bianet Castellanos is associate professor of American studies at the University of Minnesota. She works with Maya communities in Cancún and Los Angeles. She is the author of *A Return to Servitude: Maya Migration and the Tourist Trade in Cancún* (University of Minnesota Press, 2010) and co-editor of *Comparative Indigeneities of the Américas: Toward a Hemispheric Approach* (with Lourdes Gutiérrez Nájera and Arturo Aldama, University of Arizona Press, 2012). She edited a forum on settler colonialism in Latin America for *American Quarterly* (2017) and contributed to a special issue on critical Latinx indigeneities for *Latino Studies* (2018). She is currently working on a monograph on housing and Indigenous urbanism in Mexico.

Juan Antonio Flores Martos is associate professor of social anthropology at the University of Castilla-La Mancha, Talavera de la Reina. He is editor-in-chief of *AIBR: Revista de Antropología Iberoamericana*. His research focuses on ethnographies of the body, emotion, ritual, and spiritual imaginaries in Bolivia, Spain, and the port of Veracruz, Mexico. In 2012, he was appointed Gonzalo Aguirre Beltrán Anthropology Research Chair by the University of Veracruz and CIESAS (Centro de Investigaciones y Estudios Superiores en Antropología Social). He has published widely on Carnival, Santa Muerte, and various aspects of folk religion in Latin America. His publication "Dances of Death in Latin América: Holy, Adopted and Patrimonialized Dead" is forthcoming in *La Santa Muerte in Mexico: History, Devotion, and Society* (edited by Wil G. Pansters, University of New Mexico Press, 2019).

Barbara Kastelein is a writer and journalist based in the United Kingdom. After completing her PhD on postfeminism and popular culture at the University of Warwick in 1994, she lived for fourteen years in Mexico City. There, she worked as a travel and environmental reporter for the *Mexico City Times* and the *Toronto Star* as well as a number of other publications. Kastelein's book *Heroes of the Pacific: The Untold Story of Acapulco's Cliff Divers* is forthcoming with Trilce Ediciones, Mexico City.

Misha Klein is associate professor of anthropology at the University of Oklahoma, where she is also affiliated with women's and gender studies, Judaic studies, and international and area studies, and she is the chair of the Clyde Snow Social Justice Award Committee. Based on ethnographic research in Brazil, her book *Kosher Feijoada and Other Paradoxes of Jewish Life in São Paulo* (University Press of Florida, 2012) explores the intersecting meanings of race, class, and belonging for the transnational and multicultural Jewish population in Brazil. She is currently conducting collaborative, interdisciplinary research in Brazil on the changing concept of race; the country's turn to the right; transnational discourses on race, Zionism, and anti-Semitism; and the implications for progressive activists.

Ellen Moodie, associate professor of anthropology at the University of Illinois at Urbana-Champaign, has been studying transitions to democracy in Central America since the end of the Cold War. Her monograph *El Salvador in the Aftermath of Peace: Crime, Uncertainty, and the Transition to Democracy* (University of Pennsylvania Press, 2010) follows the circulation of the phrase "It's worse than the war" in the years since that country's civil war ended in 1992. She is currently finishing a manuscript on middle-class and youth activism and political subjectivity in Central America, asking how politics and social relations are changing with the coming of age of the post-postwar generation—of young people with no direct memory of the armed conflicts of the past.

Fernando de Sousa Rocha is associate professor of Luso-Hispanic studies at Middlebury College, Vermont. He earned his PhD in comparative literature at the University of Southern California, Los Angeles. He is the author of *Subaltern Writings: Readings on Graciliano Ramos's Novels* (Peter Lang, 2013), which analyzes how the Brazilian author reevaluates the status of writings by subalterns. His ongoing research focuses on representations of slavery in nineteenth-century Brazilian literature, contrasting slavish textualities and Afro-Brazilian epistemologies. He has published on different topics on Brazilian literature and culture, both in the United States and abroad.

Gina Athena Ulysse is a feminist artist-anthropologist-activist, or self-described post-Zora interventionist. She is a professor of anthropology at Wesleyan University. Her research questions culminate at the intersections of geopolitics, historical representations, and the dailiness of Black diasporic conditions. She is the author of *Downtown Ladies* (University of Chicago Press, 2008), a study of informal commercial importers in Jamaica; *Why Haiti Needs New Narratives: A Post Quake Chronicle* (Wesleyan University Press, 2015), a trilingual publication in English, Kreyòl, and French; and *Because When God Is Too Busy: Haiti, me & THE WORLD* (Wesleyan University Press, 2017), a collection of photographs, poetry, and performance texts. She was the invited editor of "Caribbean Rasanblaj" (2015), a double issue of New York University's *e-misférica*. Her recent creative projects include the spoken-word meditations "BlackLiberationMashUp" (2017) and "Remixed Ode to Rebel's Spirit" (2018).

Index

Italics are used to indicate figures and illustrations. References for notes include page number and note number, e.g. 143n3.

Perez, Daniella, 27–28
Perez, Gloria, 27, 29
Petite, Jacqueline, 76, 79, 85
photography, 152–153, 163n9
Ponceele, Father Rogelio, 128–129
Portuguese people, 150–151
postcards, 153. *see also* photography
Presley, Elvis, 73, 78–79
privilege: class, 33–36; effects on ethnography, 10 (*see also* ethnography); effects on self-presentation, 32, 33–34, 41; linguistic, 32; of nationality, 31–32, 33–36, 143n9; questioning and challenging, 8, 10, 82–87, 172–176; racial, 32–33, 172–176. *See also* hierarchies
prostitution, 154, 156. *See also* sexuality

race: hierarchies of, 7, 11, 32–33, 113–114, 157; intersection with physical space, 47n15; tourist consumption of, 15, 169–171
racism, 10, 171–176
reality tours. *See* tourism
Re Cruz, Alicia, 111
Redfield, Robert, 111
residential areas, 6, 39–40, 48n22, 103, 107. *See also* housing
return, 12–14, 44–45, 91–96, 97–102; politics of, 4, 15–16
Rio de Janeiro, *151, 156, 157, 159, 160*; exploring the spaces of, 14–15, 147–163; fortresses of, 150–152; historical sites of, 150–152, 156–157
risk, 9, 91, 96–97. *See also* violence; vulnerability
Robben, Antonius C. G. M., 9
Rocha, Fernando de Sousa (in this collection), 9–10, 14–15, 147–163
Roma, 28–29
Romero, Óscar, 134
Rosaldo, Michelle Zimbalist, 69
Rosaldo, Renato, 8, 43

Sacramento, Octávio, 54–55
Said, Edward, 3, 15
samba, 154, 160
Sánchez, Ignacio "Nacho," 75–76, 78
Sánchez, Yoani, 94–96
San Juan Guichicovi, 56–57
Santiago (Carlos Henríquez Consalvi), 130, 131, 137
São Carlos do Pinhal, 22–23
schemes, 149–150. *See also* narrative
scholars, 5, 7–12, 15, 39–41, 48n18. *See also* anthropologists; Rocha, Fernando de Sousa
Second World, 48n16
Sennett, Richard, 148
service staff, 114. *See also* domestic employees; hotels; tour guides
sexuality: in history and geopolitics, 5, 66; and the practice of ethnography, 9, 54–55, 60–61, 86; and tourism, 54–55, 74–76, 154, 156 (*see also* tourism)
Shannon (pseudonym), 123–124, 132, 135–137
Smith, Lindsey Clair, 11
Spaniards, 53–55, 60–61
Stoll, David, 127
students, 7, 13, 93–94, 100–102
Sugarloaf Mountain, 152, 157–158, *159,* 163n18

The Gift, 84–85
Third World, 48n16
tour guides, 149. *See also* Esmeralda; Márquez, Raquel
tourism: as cultural imperialism, 3–5; economies of, 6–7; ecotourism, 105–106, 115, 118–119; infrastructure for, 114–116 (*see also* airports; hotels); reality tours, 6, 42–43, 48n22; schemes of, 149–150; sexuality and, 54–55, 74–76 (*see also* sexuality); sites of, 147–163, 157–158; solidarity tourism, 14, 122–145; transformative potentials of, 129, 161–162, 170